Feasting at Wisdom's Table

Compiled by Joseph Lumpkin

Feasting at Wisdom's Table

First time or interested authors, contact Fifth Estate Publishers, Post Office Box 116, Blountsville, AL 35031.

First Printing 2009

Cover Design by An Quigley

Printed on acid-free paper

Library of Congress Control No: 2009902866

ISBN: 9781933580586
1933580585

Fifth Estate 2009

Introduction

The search for wisdom has been the pole-star of humanity for six thousand years. Religions have come and gone, philosophies have failed, but those surviving wells of wisdom go deep and yield sweet refreshment for the soul.

Buddhism, Taoism, Hinduism, Zen, and Eastern Christian writings have served as pathways to peace and enlightenment, but the path is not easily traveled. Wisdom is a harsh master, demanding authenticity and truth. No self-delusion or protection will be tolerated. The seeker must be spiritually eviscerated. Mind and soul must be laid bare. Toward this end, pilgrims have followed teachings within a handful of ancient books.

Now, the greatest books of Eastern wisdom are brought together for the sake of those seeking the path of enlightenment and liberation.

Buddhism

Gautama or Siddhartha Buddha or 'The Enlightened One' was born into a wealthy Kshatriya family, in Lumbini, at the foothills of Nepal around 566 B.C. He founded the religion of Buddhism after attaining "enlightenment," having set in meditation under a tree at Bodhgaya for a period of time. Buddha died around 486 B.C.

The main spiritual goal of Buddhism is to attain "Enlightenment" or 'Nirvana', in which one attains the spiritual liberation from the cycle of birth and rebirth.

Buddhism does not concern itself with the existence of god. Its approach and ceremonies are simple and direct. Its philosophy is that every one is equal, life is transient, and nothing happens by chance.

In Buddha's first public address he charted a path to enlightenment containing what he called "The four noble truths," which are:

1. The world is full of suffering.
2. Suffering is caused by desire.
3. Suffering can be removed.

4. To stop suffering, overcome desire.

According to Buddha these noble truths can be achieved by following the 'eight fold path', comprised of:

1. Right view.
2. Right thought.
3. Right speech.
4. Right action.
5. Right livelihood.
6. Right effort.
7. Right mindfulness.
8. Right concentration.

One of Buddhism's most important documents is The Sermon at Benares, entitled, the *Dhammacakkappavattanasutra,* "The Turning of the Wheel of Dharma." This sermon is to Buddhist religion what "The Sermon on the Mount" is to the Christian religion. It proclaims the first and central teachings.

Dharma is the religious doctrine making up the rights and duties of the individual. It is the righteous duty and the virtuous path or act flowing there from. Because it is the act flowing from one's belief, it contextually implies one's religion.

The sayings of the Buddha were extracted out of the stories of Buddha's life from *The Dhammapada*, which means "the path of dharma." This book consists of 423 sayings of the Buddha, grouped into 26 categories. The sayings of the Buddha were not meant to be a fixed doctrine. In Buddhism there is no set canon. Anyone, having attained enlightenment, can add to the body of work. It is up to the teacher or individuals to accept or reject the individual teachings. Instead, it could be said that the writings of any Buddha are observations on the path and provide insights for the seeker.

Presented here are the entire 423 verses, translated by Friedrich Max Müller, a *German scholar,* born Dec. 6, 1823, Dessau, duchy of Anhalt, Germany, died Oct. 28, 1900, Oxford, England.

To aid the reader, there is a short glossary of terms included at the end of the text, beginning on page 68.

The Dhammapada

A Collection of Verses

Being One of the Canonical Books of the Buddhists

Translated from Pali by F. Max Muller

From: The Sacred Books of the East, Translated by Various Oriental Scholars, Edited by F. Max Muller. Volume X Part I

Chapter I The Twin-Verses

1. All that we are is the result of what we have thought: it is founded on our thoughts, it is made up of our thoughts. If a man speaks or acts with an evil thought, pain follows him, as the wheel follows the foot of the ox that draws the carriage.

2. All that we are is the result of what we have thought: it is founded on our thoughts, it is made up of our thoughts. If a man speaks or acts with a pure thought, happiness follows him, like a shadow that never leaves him.

3. "He abused me, he beat me, he defeated me, he robbed me," —in those who harbor such thoughts hatred will never cease.

4. "He abused me, he beat me, he defeated me, he robbed me," —in those who do not harbor such thoughts hatred will cease.

5. For hatred does not cease by hatred at any time: hatred ceases by love, this is an old rule.

6. The world does not know that we must all come to an end here;— but those who know it, their quarrels cease at once.

7. He who lives looking for pleasures only, his senses uncontrolled, immoderate in his food, idle, and weak, Mara (the tempter) will certainly overthrow him, as the wind throws down a weak tree.

8. He who lives without looking for pleasures, his senses well controlled, moderate in his food, faithful and strong, him Mara will certainly not overthrow, any more than the wind throws down a rocky mountain.

9. He who wishes to put on the yellow dress without having cleansed himself from sin, who disregards temperance and truth, is unworthy of the yellow dress.

10. But he who has cleansed himself from sin, is well grounded in all virtues, and regards also temperance and truth, he is indeed worthy of the yellow dress.

11. They who imagine truth in untruth, and see untruth in truth,

never arrive at truth, but follow vain desires.

12. They who know truth in truth, and untruth in untruth, arrive at truth, and follow true desires.

13. As rain breaks through an ill-thatched house, passion will break through an unreflecting mind.

14. As rain does not break through a well-thatched house, passion will not break through a well-reflecting mind.

15. The evil-doer mourns in this world, and he mourns in the next; he mourns in both. He mourns and suffers when he sees the evil of his own work.

16. The virtuous man delights in this world, and he delights in the next; he delights in both. He delights and rejoices, when he sees the purity of his own work.

17. The evil-doer suffers in this world, and he suffers in the next; he suffers in both. He suffers when he thinks of the evil he has done; he suffers more when going on the evil path.

18. The virtuous man is happy in this world, and he is happy in the next; he is happy in both. He is happy when he thinks of the good he has done; he is still more happy when going on the good path.

19. The thoughtless man, even if he can recite a large portion (of the

law), but is not a doer of it, has no share in the priesthood, but is like a cowherd counting the cows of others.

20. The follower of the law, even if he can recite only a small portion (of the law), but, having forsaken passion and hatred and foolishness, possesses true knowledge and serenity of mind, he, caring for nothing in this world or that to come, has indeed a share in the priesthood.

Chapter II On Earnestness

21. Earnestness is the path of immortality (Nirvana), thoughtlessness the path of death. Those who are in earnest do not die, those who are thoughtless are as if dead already.

22. Those who are advanced in earnestness, having understood this clearly, delight in earnestness, and rejoice in the knowledge of the Ariyas (the elect).

23. These wise people, meditative, steady, always possessed of strong powers, attain to Nirvana, the highest happiness.

24. If an earnest person has roused himself, if he is not forgetful, if his deeds are pure, if he acts with consideration, if he restrains himself, and lives according to law,—then his glory will increase.

25. By rousing himself, by earnestness, by restraint and control, the

wise man may make for himself an island which no flood can overwhelm.

26. Fools follow after vanity, men of evil wisdom. The wise man keeps earnestness as his best jewel.

27. Follow not after vanity, nor after the enjoyment of love and lust! He who is earnest and meditative, obtains ample joy.

28. When the learned man drives away vanity by earnestness, he, the wise, climbing the terraced heights of wisdom, looks down upon the fools, serene he looks upon the toiling crowd, as one that stands on a mountain looks down upon them that stand upon the plain.

29. Earnest among the thoughtless, awake among the sleepers, the wise man advances like a racer, leaving behind the hack.

30. By earnestness did Maghavan (Indra) rise to the lordship of the gods. People praise earnestness; thoughtlessness is always blamed.

31. A Bhikshu (mendicant) who delights in earnestness, who looks with fear on thoughtlessness, moves about like fire, burning all his fetters, small or large.

32. A Bhikshu (mendicant) who delights in reflection, who looks with fear on thoughtlessness, cannot fall away (from his perfect state)—he is close upon Nirvana.

Chapter III Thought

33. As a fletcher makes straight his arrow, a wise man makes straight his trembling and unsteady thought, which is difficult to guard, difficult to hold back.

34. As a fish taken from his watery home and thrown on dry ground, our thought trembles all over in order to escape the dominion of Mara (the tempter).

35. It is good to tame the mind, which is difficult to hold in and flighty, rushing wherever it wants to go; a tamed mind brings happiness.

36. Let the wise man guard his thoughts, for they are difficult to perceive, very artful, and they rush wherever they list: thoughts well guarded bring happiness.

37. Those who bridle their mind which travels far, moves about alone, is without a body, and hides in the chamber (of the heart), will be free from the bonds of Mara (the tempter).

38. If a man's thoughts are unsteady, if he does not know the true law, if his peace of mind is troubled, his knowledge will never be perfect.

39. If a man's thoughts are not dissipated, if his mind is not

perplexed, if he has ceased to think of good or evil, then there is no fear for him while he is watchful.

40. Knowing that this body is (fragile) like a jar, and making this thought firm like a fortress, one should attack Mara (the tempter) with the weapon of knowledge, one should watch him when conquered, and should never rest.

41. Before long, alas! this body will lie on the earth, despised, without understanding, like a useless log.

42. Whatever a hater may do to a hater, or an enemy to an enemy, a wrongly-directed mind will do us greater mischief.

43. Not a mother, not a father will do so much, nor any other relative; a well-directed mind will do us greater service.

Chapter IV Flowers

44. Who shall overcome this earth, and the world of Yama (the lord of the departed), and the world of the gods? Who shall find out the plainly shown path of virtue, as a clever man finds out the (right) flower?

45. The disciple will overcome the earth, and the world of Yama, and the world of the gods. The disciple will find out the plainly shown path of virtue, as a clever man finds out the (right) flower.

46. He who knows that this body is like froth, and has learnt that it is as unsubstantial as a mirage, will break the flower-pointed arrow of Mara, and never see the king of death.

47. Death carries off a man who is gathering flowers and whose mind is distracted, as a flood carries off a sleeping village.

48. Death subdues a man who is gathering flowers, and whose mind is distracted, before he is satiated in his pleasures.

49. As the bee collects nectar and departs without injuring the flower, or its color or scent, so let a sage dwell in his village.

50. Not the perversities of others, not their sins of commission or omission, but his own misdeeds and negligence should a sage take notice of.

51. Like a beautiful flower, full of color, but without scent, are the fine but fruitless words of him who does not act accordingly.

52. But, like a beautiful flower, full of color and full of scent, are the fine and fruitful words of him who acts accordingly.

53. As many kinds of wreaths can be made from a heap of flowers, so many good things may be achieved by a mortal when once he is born.

54. The scent of flowers does not travel against the wind, nor (that of)

sandal-wood, or of Tagara and Mallika flowers; but the odor of good people travels even against the wind; a good man pervades every place.

55. Sandal-wood or Tagara, a lotus-flower, or a Vassiki, among these sorts of perfumes, the perfume of virtue is unsurpassed.

56. Mean is the scent that comes from Tagara and sandal-wood;—the perfume of those who possess virtue rises up to the gods as the highest.

57. Of the people who possess these virtues, who live without thoughtlessness, and who are emancipated through true knowledge, Mara, the tempter, never finds the way.

58, 59. As on a heap of rubbish cast upon the highway the lily will grow full of sweet perfume and delight, thus the disciple of the truly enlightened Buddha shines forth by his knowledge among those who are like rubbish, among the people that walk in darkness.

Chapter V The Fool

60. Long is the night to him who is awake; long is a mile to him who is tired; long is life to the foolish who do not know the true law.

61. If a traveler does not meet with one who is his better, or his equal, let him firmly keep to his solitary journey; there is no companionship

with a fool.

62. "These sons belong to me, and this wealth belongs to me," with such thoughts a fool is tormented. He himself does not belong to himself; how much less sons and wealth?

63. The fool who knows his foolishness, is wise at least so far. But a fool who thinks himself wise, he is called a fool indeed.

64. If a fool be associated with a wise man even all his life, he will perceive the truth as little as a spoon perceives the taste of soup.

65. If an intelligent man be associated for one minute only with a wise man, he will soon perceive the truth, as the tongue perceives the taste of soup.

66. Fools of little understanding have themselves for their greatest enemies, for they do evil deeds which must bear bitter fruits.

67. That deed is not well done of which a man must repent, and the reward of which he receives crying and with a tearful face.

68. No, that deed is well done of which a man does not repent, and the reward of which he receives gladly and cheerfully.

69. As long as the evil deed done does not bear fruit, the fool thinks it is like honey; but when it ripens, then the fool suffers grief.

70. Let a fool month after month eat his food (like an ascetic) with the tip of a blade of Kusa grass, yet he is not worth the sixteenth particle of those who have well weighed the law.

71. An evil deed, like newly-drawn milk, does not turn (suddenly); smoldering, like fire covered by ashes, it follows the fool.

72. And when the evil deed, after it has become known, brings sorrow to the fool, then it destroys his bright lot, nay, it cleaves his head.

73. Let the fool wish for a false reputation, for precedence among the Bhikshus, for lordship in the convents, for worship among other people!

74. "May both the layman and he who has left the world think that this is done by me; may they be subject to me in everything which is to be done or is not to be done," thus is the mind of the fool, and his desire and pride increase.

75. "One is the road that leads to wealth, another the road that leads to Nirvana;" if the Bhikshu, the disciple of Buddha, has learnt this, he will not yearn for honor, he will strive after separation from the world.

Chapter VI The Wise Man (Pandita)

76. If you see an intelligent man who tells you where true treasures are to be found, who shows what is to be avoided, and administers reproofs, follow that wise man; it will be better, not worse, for those who follow him.

77. Let him admonish, let him teach, let him forbid what is improper!- -he will be beloved of the good, by the bad he will be hated.

78. Do not have evil-doers for friends, do not have low people for friends: have virtuous people for friends, have for friends the best of men.

79. He who drinks in the law lives happily with a serene mind: the sage rejoices always in the law, as preached by the elect (Ariyas).

80. Well-makers lead the water (wherever they like); fletchers bend the arrow; carpenters bend a log of wood; wise people fashion themselves.

81. As a solid rock is not shaken by the wind, wise people falter not amidst blame and praise.

82. Wise people, after they have listened to the laws, become serene, like a deep, smooth, and still lake.

83. Good people walk on whatever befall, the good do not prattle, longing for pleasure; whether touched by happiness or sorrow wise people never appear elated or depressed.

84. If, whether for his own sake, or for the sake of others, a man wishes neither for a son, nor for wealth, nor for lordship, and if he does not wish for his own success by unfair means, then he is good, wise, and virtuous.

85. Few are there among men who arrive at the other shore (become Arhats); the other people here run up and down the shore.

86. But those who, when the law has been well preached to them, follow the law, will pass across the dominion of death, however difficult to overcome.

87, 88. A wise man should leave the dark state (of ordinary life), and follow the bright state (of the Bhikshu). After going from his home to a homeless state, he should in his retirement look for enjoyment where there seemed to be no enjoyment. Leaving all pleasures behind, and calling nothing his own, the wise man should purge himself from all the troubles of the mind.

89. Those whose mind is well grounded in the (seven) elements of

knowledge, who without clinging to anything, rejoice in freedom from attachment, whose appetites have been conquered, and who are full of light, are free (even) in this world.

Chapter VII The Venerable (Arhat).

90. There is no suffering for him who has finished his journey, and abandoned grief, who has freed himself on all sides, and thrown off all fetters.

91. They depart with their thoughts well-collected, they are not happy in their abode; like swans who have left their lake, they leave their house and home.

92. Men who have no riches, who live on recognized food, who have perceived void and unconditioned freedom (Nirvana), their path is difficult to understand, like that of birds in the air.

93. He whose appetites are stilled, who is not absorbed in enjoyment, who has perceived void and unconditioned freedom (Nirvana), his path is difficult to understand, like that of birds in the air.

94. The gods even envy him whose senses, like horses well broken in by the driver, have been subdued, who is free from pride, and free from appetites.

95. Such a one who does his duty is tolerant like the earth, like

Indra's bolt; he is like a lake without mud; no new births are in store for him.

96. His thought is quiet, quiet are his word and deed, when he has obtained freedom by true knowledge, when he has thus become a quiet man.

97. The man who is free from credulity, but knows the uncreated, who has cut all ties, removed all temptations, renounced all desires, he is the greatest of men.

98. In a hamlet or in a forest, in the deep water or on the dry land, wherever venerable persons (Arhanta) dwell, that place is delightful.

99. Forests are delightful; where the world finds no delight, there the passionless will find delight, for they look not for pleasures.

Chapter VIII The Thousands

100. Even though a speech be a thousand (of words), but made up of senseless words, one word of sense is better, which if a man hears, he becomes quiet.

101. Even though a Gatha (poem) be a thousand (of words), but made up of senseless words, one word of a Gatha is better, which if a man hears, he becomes quiet.

102. Though a man recite a hundred Gathas made up of senseless words, one word of the law is better, which if a man hears, he becomes quiet.

103. If one man conquer in battle a thousand times thousand men, and if another conquer himself, he is the greatest of conquerors.

104, 105. One's own self conquered is better than all other people; not even a god, a Gandharva, not Mara with Brahman could change into defeat the victory of a man who has vanquished himself, and always lives under restraint.

106. If a man for a hundred years sacrifice month after month with a thousand, and if he but for one moment pay homage to a man whose soul is grounded (in true knowledge), better is that homage than sacrifice for a hundred years.

107. If a man for a hundred years worship Agni (fire) in the forest, and if he but for one moment pay homage to a man whose soul is grounded (in true knowledge), better is that homage than sacrifice for a hundred years.

108. Whatever a man sacrifice in this world as an offering or as an oblation for a whole year in order to gain merit, the whole of it is not worth a quarter (a farthing); reverence shown to the righteous is better.

109. He who always greets and constantly reveres the aged, four things will increase to him, viz. life, beauty, happiness, power.

110. But he who lives a hundred years, vicious and unrestrained, a life of one day is better if a man is virtuous and reflecting.

111. And he who lives a hundred years, ignorant and unrestrained, a life of one day is better if a man is wise and reflecting.

112. And he who lives a hundred years, idle and weak, a life of one day is better if a man has attained firm strength.

113. And he who lives a hundred years, not seeing beginning and end, a life of one day is better if a man sees beginning and end.

114. And he who lives a hundred years, not seeing the immortal place, a life of one day is better if a man sees the immortal place.

115. And he who lives a hundred years, not seeing the highest law, a life of one day is better if a man sees the highest law.

Chapter IX Evil

116. If a man would hasten towards the good, he should keep his thought away from evil; if a man does what is good slothfully, his mind delights in evil.

117. If a man commits a sin, let him not do it again; let him not

delight in sin: pain is the outcome of evil.

118. If a man does what is good, let him do it again; let him delight in it: happiness is the outcome of good.

119. Even an evil-doer sees happiness as long as his evil deed has not ripened; but when his evil deed has ripened, then does the evil-doer see evil.

120. Even a good man sees evil days, as long as his good deed has not ripened; but when his good deed has ripened, then does the good man see happy days.

121. Let no man think lightly of evil, saying in his heart, It will not come nigh unto me. Even by the falling of water-drops a water-pot is filled; the fool becomes full of evil, even if he gather it little by little.

122. Let no man think lightly of good, saying in his heart, It will not come nigh unto me. Even by the falling of water-drops a water-pot is filled; the wise man becomes full of good, even if he gather it little by little.

123. Let a man avoid evil deeds, as a merchant, if he has few companions and carries much wealth, avoids a dangerous road; as a man who loves life avoids poison.

124. He who has no wound on his hand, may touch poison with his

hand; poison does not affect one who has no wound; nor is there evil for one who does not commit evil.

125. If a man offend a harmless, pure, and innocent person, the evil falls back upon that fool, like light dust thrown up against the wind.

126. Some people are born again; evil-doers go to hell; righteous people go to heaven; those who are free from all worldly desires attain Nirvana.

127. Not in the sky, not in the midst of the sea, not if we enter into the clefts of the mountains, is there known a spot in the whole world where death could not overcome (the mortal).

Chapter X Punishment

129. All men tremble at punishment, all men fear death; remember that you are like unto them, and do not kill, nor cause slaughter.

130. All men tremble at punishment, all men love life; remember that thou art like unto them, and do not kill, nor cause slaughter.

131. He who seeking his own happiness punishes or kills beings who also long for happiness, will not find happiness after death.

132. He who seeking his own happiness does not punish or kill beings who also long for happiness, will find happiness after death.

133. Do not speak harshly to anybody; those who are spoken to will answer thee in the same way. Angry speech is painful, blows for blows will touch thee.

134. If, like a shattered metal plate (gong), thou utter not, then thou hast reached Nirvana; contention is not known to thee.

135. As a cowherd with his staff drives his cows into the stable, so do Age and Death drive the life of men.

136. A fool does not know when he commits his evil deeds: but the wicked man burns by his own deeds, as if burnt by fire.

137. He who inflicts pain on innocent and harmless persons, will soon come to one of these ten states:

138. He will have cruel suffering, loss, injury of the body, heavy affliction, or loss of mind,

139. Or a misfortune coming from the king, or a fearful accusation, or loss of relations, or destruction of treasures,

140. Or lightning-fire will burn his houses; and when his body is destroyed, the fool will go to hell.

141. Not nakedness, not platted hair, not dirt, not fasting, or lying on the earth, not rubbing with dust, not sitting motionless, can purify a mortal who has not overcome desires.

142. He who, though dressed in fine apparel, exercises tranquility, is quiet, subdued, restrained, chaste, and has ceased to find fault with all other beings, he indeed is a Brahmana, an ascetic (sramana), a friar (bhikshu).

143. Is there in this world any man so restrained by humility that he does not mind reproof, as a well-trained horse the whip?

144. Like a well-trained horse when touched by the whip, be ye active and lively, and by faith, by virtue, by energy, by meditation, by discernment of the law you will overcome this great pain (of reproof), perfect in knowledge and in behavior, and never forgetful.

145. Well-makers lead the water (wherever they like); fletchers bend the arrow; carpenters bend a log of wood; good people fashion themselves.

Chapter XI Old Age

146. How is there laughter, how is there joy, as this world is always burning? Why do you not seek a light, ye who are surrounded by darkness?

147. Look at this dressed-up lump, covered with wounds, joined together, sickly, full of many thoughts, which has no strength, no hold!

148. This body is wasted, full of sickness, and frail; this heap of corruption breaks to pieces, life indeed ends in death.

149. Those white bones, like gourds thrown away in the autumn, what pleasure is there in looking at them?

150. After a stronghold has been made of the bones, it is covered with flesh and blood, and there dwell in it old age and death, pride and deceit.

151. The brilliant chariots of kings are destroyed, the body also approaches destruction, but the virtue of good people never approaches destruction,—thus do the good say to the good.

152. A man who has learnt little, grows old like an ox; his flesh grows, but his knowledge does not grow.

153, 154. Looking for the maker of this tabernacle, I shall have to run through a course of many births, so long as I do not find (him); and painful is birth again and again. But now, maker of the tabernacle, thou hast been seen; you shall not make up this tabernacle again. All thy rafters are broken, thy ridge-pole is sundered; the mind, approaching the Eternal (visankhara, nirvana), has attained to the extinction of all desires.

155. Men who have not observed proper discipline, and have not gained treasure in their youth, perish like old herons in a lake

without fish.

156. Men who have not observed proper discipline, and have not gained treasure in their youth, lie, like broken bows, sighing after the past.

Chapter XII Self

157. If a man hold himself dear, let him watch himself carefully; during one at least out of the three watches a wise man should be watchful.

158. Let each man direct himself first to what is proper, then let him teach others; thus a wise man will not suffer.

159. If a man make himself as he teaches others to be, then, being himself well subdued, he may subdue (others); one's own self is indeed difficult to subdue.

160. Self is the lord of self, who else could be the lord? With self well subdued, a man finds a lord such as few can find.

161. The evil done by oneself, self-begotten, self-bred, crushes the foolish, as a diamond breaks a precious stone.

162. He whose wickedness is very great brings himself down to that state where his enemy wishes him to be, as a creeper does with the

tree which it surrounds.

163. Bad deeds, and deeds hurtful to ourselves, are easy to do; what is beneficial and good, that is very difficult to do.

164. The foolish man who scorns the rule of the venerable (Arahat), of the elect (Ariya), of the virtuous, and follows false doctrine, he bears fruit to his own destruction, like the fruits of the Katthaka reed.

165. By oneself the evil is done, by oneself one suffers; by oneself evil is left undone, by oneself one is purified. Purity and impurity belong to oneself, no one can purify another.

166. Let no one forget his own duty for the sake of another's, however great; let a man, after he has discerned his own duty, be always attentive to his duty.

Chapter XIII The World

167. Do not follow the evil law! Do not live on in thoughtlessness! Do not follow false doctrine! Be not a friend of the world.

168. Rouse thyself! do not be idle! Follow the law of virtue! The virtuous rests in bliss in this world and in the next.

169. Follow the law of virtue; do not follow that of sin. The virtuous rests in bliss in this world and in the next.

170. Look upon the world as a bubble, look upon it as a mirage: the king of death does not see him who thus looks down upon the world.

171. Come, look at this glittering world, like unto a royal chariot; the foolish are immersed in it, but the wise do not touch it.

172. He who formerly was reckless and afterwards became sober, brightens up this world, like the moon when freed from clouds.

173. He whose evil deeds are covered by good deeds, brightens up this world, like the moon when freed from clouds.

174. This world is dark, few only can see here; a few only go to heaven, like birds escaped from the net.

175. The swans go on the path of the sun, they go through the ether by means of their miraculous power; the wise are led out of this world, when they have conquered Mara and his train.

176. If a man has transgressed one law, and speaks lies, and scoffs at another world, there is no evil he will not do.

177. The uncharitable do not go to the world of the gods; fools only do not praise liberality; a wise man rejoices in liberality, and through it becomes blessed in the other world.

178. Better than sovereignty over the earth, better than going to heaven, better than lordship over all worlds, is the reward of the first

step in holiness.

Chapter XIV The Buddha (The Awakened)

179. He whose conquest is not conquered again, into whose conquest no one in this world enters, by what track can you lead him, the Awakened, the Omniscient, the trackless?

180. He whom no desire with its snares and poisons can lead astray, by what track can you lead him, the Awakened, the Omniscient, the trackless?

181. Even the gods envy those who are awakened and not forgetful, who are given to meditation, who are wise, and who delight in the repose of retirement (from the world).

182. Difficult (to obtain) is the conception of men, difficult is the life of mortals, difficult is the hearing of the True Law, difficult is the birth of the Awakened (the attainment of Buddhahood).

183. Not to commit any sin, to do good, and to purify one's mind, that is the teaching of (all) the Awakened.

184. The Awakened call patience the highest penance, long-suffering the highest Nirvana; for he is not an anchorite (pravragita) who strikes others, he is not an ascetic (sramana) who insults others.

185. Not to blame, not to strike, to live restrained under the law, to be moderate in eating, to sleep and sit alone, and to dwell on the highest thoughts,—this is the teaching of the Awakened.

186. There is no satisfying lusts, even by a shower of gold pieces; he who knows that lusts have a short taste and cause pain, he is wise;

187. Even in heavenly pleasures he finds no satisfaction, the disciple who is fully awakened delights only in the destruction of all desires.

188. Men, driven by fear, go to many a refuge, to mountains and forests, to groves and sacred trees.

189. But that is not a safe refuge, that is not the best refuge; a man is not delivered from all pains after having gone to that refuge.

190. He who takes refuge with Buddha, the Law, and the Church; he who, with clear understanding, sees the four holy truths:—

191. Viz. pain, the origin of pain, the destruction of pain, and the eightfold holy way that leads to the quieting of pain;—

192. That is the safe refuge, that is the best refuge; having gone to that refuge, a man is delivered from all pain.

193. A supernatural person (a Buddha) is not easily found, he is not born everywhere. Wherever such a sage is born, that race prospers.

194. Happy is the arising of the awakened, happy is the teaching of the True Law, happy is peace in the church, happy is the devotion of those who are at peace.

195, 196. He who pays homage to those who deserve homage, whether the awakened (Buddha) or their disciples, those who have overcome the host (of evils), and crossed the flood of sorrow, he who pays homage to such as have found deliverance and know no fear, his merit can never be measured by anybody.

Chapter XV Happiness

197. Let us live happily then, not hating those who hate us! among men who hate us let us dwell free from hatred!

198. Let us live happily then, free from ailments among the ailing! among men who are ailing let us dwell free from ailments!

199. Let us live happily then, free from greed among the greedy! among men who are greedy let us dwell free from greed!

200. Let us live happily then, though we call nothing our own! We shall be like the bright gods, feeding on happiness!

201. Victory breeds hatred, for the conquered is unhappy. He who has given up both victory and defeat, he, the contented, is happy.

202. There is no fire like passion; there is no losing throw like hatred; there is no pain like this body; there is no happiness higher than rest.

203. Hunger is the worst of diseases, the body the greatest of pains; if one knows this truly, that is Nirvana, the highest happiness.

204. Health is the greatest of gifts, contentedness the best riches; trust is the best of relationships, Nirvana the highest happiness.

205. He who has tasted the sweetness of solitude and tranquility, is free from fear and free from sin, while he tastes the sweetness of drinking in the law.

206. The sight of the elect (Arya) is good, to live with them is always happiness; if a man does not see fools, he will be truly happy.

207. He who walks in the company of fools suffers a long way; company with fools, as with an enemy, is always painful; company with the wise is pleasure, like meeting with kinsfolk.

208. Therefore, one ought to follow the wise, the intelligent, the learned, the much enduring, the dutiful, the elect; one ought to follow a good and wise man, as the moon follows the path of the stars.

Chapter XVI Pleasure

209. He who gives himself to vanity, and does not give himself to meditation, forgetting the real aim (of life) and grasping at pleasure, will in time envy him who has exerted himself in meditation.

210. Let no man ever look for what is pleasant, or what is unpleasant. Not to see what is pleasant is pain, and it is pain to see what is unpleasant.

211. Let, therefore, no man love anything; loss of the beloved is evil. Those who love nothing and hate nothing, have no fetters.

212. From pleasure comes grief, from pleasure comes fear; he who is free from pleasure knows neither grief nor fear.

213. From affection comes grief, from affection comes fear; he who is free from affection knows neither grief nor fear.

214. From lust comes grief, from lust comes fear; he who is free from lust knows neither grief nor fear.

215. From love comes grief, from love comes fear; he who is free from love knows neither grief nor fear.

216. From greed comes grief, from greed comes fear; he who is free

from greed knows neither grief nor fear.

217. He who possesses virtue and intelligence, who is just, speaks the truth, and does what is his own business, him the world will hold dear.

218. He in whom a desire for the Ineffable (Nirvana) has sprung up, who is satisfied in his mind, and whose thoughts are not bewildered by love, he is called urdhvamsrotas (carried upwards by the stream).

219. Kinsmen, friends, and lovers salute a man who has been long away, and returns safe from afar.

220. In like manner his good works receive him who has done good, and has gone from this world to the other;—as kinsmen receive a friend on his return.

Chapter XVII Anger

221. Let a man leave anger, let him forsake pride, let him overcome all bondage! No sufferings befall the man who is not attached to name and form, and who calls nothing his own.

222. He who holds back rising anger like a rolling chariot, him I call a real driver; other people are but holding the reins.

223. Let a man overcome anger by love, let him overcome evil by

good; let him overcome the greedy by liberality, the liar by truth!

224. Speak the truth, do not yield to anger; give, if thou art asked for little; by these three steps thou wilt go near the gods.

225. The sages who injure nobody, and who always control their body, they will go to the unchangeable place (Nirvana), where, if they have gone, they will suffer no more.

226. Those who are ever watchful, who study day and night, and who strive after Nirvana, their passions will come to an end.

227. This is an old saying, O Atula, this is not only of to-day: 'They blame him who sits silent, they blame him who speaks much, they also blame him who says little; there is no one on earth who is not blamed.'

228. There never was, there never will be, nor is there now, a man who is always blamed, or a man who is always praised.

229, 230. But he whom those who discriminate praise continually day after day, as without blemish, wise, rich in knowledge and virtue, who would dare to blame him, like a coin made of gold from the Gambu river? Even the gods praise him, he is praised even by Brahman.

231. Beware of bodily anger, and control thy body! Leave the sins of

the body, and with thy body practice virtue!

232. Beware of the anger of the tongue, and control thy tongue! Leave the sins of the tongue, and practice virtue with thy tongue!

233. Beware of the anger of the mind, and control thy mind! Leave the sins of the mind, and practice virtue with thy mind!

234. The wise who control their body, who control their tongue, the wise who control their mind, are indeed well controlled.

Chapter XVIII Impurity

235. Thou art now like a sear leaf, the messengers of death (Yama) have come near to thee; you stand at the door of thy departure, and thou hast no provision for thy journey.

236. Make thyself an island, work hard, be wise! When thy impurities are blown away, and thou art free from guilt, thou wilt enter into the heavenly world of the elect (Ariya).

237. Thy life has come to an end, thou art come near to death (Yama), there is no resting-place for thee on the road, and thou hast no provision for thy journey.

238. Make thyself an island, work hard, be wise! When thy impurities are blown away, and thou art free from guilt, thou wilt not enter

again into birth and decay.

239. Let a wise man blow off the impurities of his self, as a smith blows off the impurities of silver one by one, little by little, and from time to time.

240. As the impurity which springs from the iron, when it springs from it, destroys it; thus do a transgressor's own works lead him to the evil path.

241. The taint of prayers is non-repetition; the taint of houses, non-repair; the taint of the body is sloth; the taint of a watchman, thoughtlessness.

242. Bad conduct is the taint of woman, greediness the taint of a benefactor; tainted are all evil ways in this world and in the next.

243. But there is a taint worse than all taints,—ignorance is the greatest taint. O mendicants! throw off that taint, and become taintless!

244. Life is easy to live for a man who is without shame, a crow hero, a mischief-maker, an insulting, bold, and wretched fellow.

245. But life is hard to live for a modest man, who always looks for what is pure, who is disinterested, quiet, spotless, and intelligent.

246. He who destroys life, who speaks untruth, who in this world

takes what is not given him, who goes to another man's wife;

247. And the man who gives himself to drinking intoxicating liquors, he, even in this world, digs up his own root.

248. O man, know this, that the unrestrained are in a bad state; take care that greediness and vice do not bring thee to grief for a long time!

249. The world gives according to their faith or according to their pleasure: if a man frets about the food and the drink given to others, he will find no rest either by day or by night.

250. He in whom that feeling is destroyed, and taken out with the very root, finds rest by day and by night.

251. There is no fire like passion, there is no shark like hatred, there is no snare like folly, there is no torrent like greed.

252. The fault of others is easily perceived, but that of oneself is difficult to perceive; a man winnows his neighbor's faults like chaff, but his own fault he hides, as a cheat hides the bad die from the gambler.

253. If a man looks after the faults of others, and is always inclined to be offended, his own passions will grow, and he is far from the destruction of passions.

254. There is no path through the air, a man is not a Samana by outward acts. The world delights in vanity, the Tathagatas (the Buddhas) are free from vanity.

255. There is no path through the air, a man is not a Samana by outward acts. No creatures are eternal; but the awakened (Buddha) are never shaken.

Chapter XIX The Just

256, 257. A man is not just if he carries a matter by violence; no, he who distinguishes both right and wrong, who is learned and leads others, not by violence, but by law and equity, and who is guarded by the law and intelligent, he is called just.

258. A man is not learned because he talks much; he who is patient, free from hatred and fear, he is called learned.

259. A man is not a supporter of the law because he talks much; even if a man has learnt little, but sees the law bodily, he is a supporter of the law, a man who never neglects the law.

260. A man is not an elder because his head is grey; his age may be ripe, but he is called 'Old-in-vain.'

261. He in whom there is truth, virtue, love, restraint, moderation, he who is free from impurity and is wise, he is called an elder.

262. An envious greedy, dishonest man does not become respectable by means of much talking only, or by the beauty of his complexion.

263. He in whom all this is destroyed, and taken out with the very root, he, when freed from hatred and wise, is called respectable.

264. Not by tonsure does an undisciplined man who speaks falsehood become a Samana; can a man be a Samana who is still held captive by desire and greediness?

265. He who always quiets the evil, whether small or large, he is called a Samana (a quiet man), because he has quieted all evil.

266. A man is not a mendicant (Bhikshu) simply because he asks others for alms; he who adopts the whole law is a Bhikshu, not he who only begs.

267. He who is above good and evil, who is chaste, who with knowledge passes through the world, he indeed is called a Bhikshu.

268, 269. A man is not a Muni because he observes silence (mona, i.e. mauna), if he is foolish and ignorant; but the wise who, taking the balance, chooses the good and avoids evil, he is a Muni, and is a Muni thereby; he who in this world weighs both sides is called a Muni.

270. A man is not an elect (Ariya) because he injures living creatures;

because he has pity on all living creatures, therefore is a man called Ariya.

271, 272. Not only by discipline and vows, not only by much learning, not by entering into a trance, not by sleeping alone, do I earn the happiness of release which no worldly person can know. Bhikshu, be not confident as long as thou hast not attained the extinction of desires.

Chapter XX The Way

273. The best of ways is the eightfold; the best of truths the four words; the best of virtues passionlessness; the best of men he who has eyes to see.

274. This is the way, there is no other that leads to the purifying of intelligence. Go on this way! Everything else is the deceit of Mara (the tempter).

275. If you go on this way, you will make an end of pain! The way was preached by me, when I had understood the removal of the thorns (in the flesh).

276. You yourself must make an effort. The Tathagatas (Buddhas) are only preachers. The thoughtful who enter the way are freed from the bondage of Mara.

277. 'All created things perish,' he who knows and sees this becomes passive in pain; this is the way to purity.

278. 'All created things are grief and pain,' he who knows and sees this becomes passive in pain; this is the way that leads to purity.

279. 'All forms are unreal,' he who knows and sees this becomes passive in pain; this is the way that leads to purity.

280. He who does not rouse himself when it is time to rise, who, though young and strong, is full of sloth, whose will and thought are weak, that lazy and idle man will never find the way to knowledge.

281. Watching his speech, well restrained in mind, let a man never commit any wrong with his body! Let a man but keep these three roads of action clear, and he will achieve the way which is taught by the wise.

282. Through zeal knowledge is gotten, through lack of zeal knowledge is lost; let a man who knows this double path of gain and loss thus place himself that knowledge may grow.

283. Cut down the whole forest (of lust), not a tree only! Danger comes out of the forest (of lust). When you have cut down both the forest (of lust) and its undergrowth, then, Bhikshus, you will be rid of the forest and free!

284. So long as the love of man towards women, even the smallest, is not destroyed, so long is his mind in bondage, as the calf that drinks milk is to its mother.

285. Cut out the love of self, like an autumn lotus, with thy hand! Cherish the road of peace. Nirvana has been shown by Sugata (Buddha).

286. 'Here I shall dwell in the rain, here in winter and summer,' thus the fool meditates, and does not think of his death.

287. Death comes and carries off that man, praised for his children and flocks, his mind distracted, as a flood carries off a sleeping village.

288. Sons are no help, nor a father, nor relations; there is no help from kinsfolk for one whom death has seized.

289. A wise and good man who knows the meaning of this, should quickly clear the way that leads to Nirvana.

Chapter XXI Miscellaneous

290. If by leaving a small pleasure one sees a great pleasure, let a wise man leave the small pleasure, and look to the great.

291. He who, by causing pain to others, wishes to obtain pleasure for

himself, he, entangled in the bonds of hatred, will never be free from hatred.

292. What ought to be done is neglected, what ought not to be done is done; the desires of unruly, thoughtless people are always increasing.

293. But they whose whole watchfulness is always directed to their body, who do not follow what ought not to be done, and who steadfastly do what ought to be done, the desires of such watchful and wise people will come to an end.

294. A true Brahmana goes scatheless, though he have killed father and mother, and two valiant kings, though he has destroyed a kingdom with all its subjects.

295. A true Brahmana goes scatheless, though he have killed father and mother, and two holy kings, and an eminent man besides.

296. The disciples of Gotama (Buddha) are always well awake, and their thoughts day and night are always set on Buddha.

297. The disciples of Gotama are always well awake, and their thoughts day and night are always set on the law.

298. The disciples of Gotama are always well awake, and their thoughts day and night are always set on the church.

299. The disciples of Gotama are always well awake, and their thoughts day and night are always set on their body.

300. The disciples of Gotama are always well awake, and their mind day and night always delights in compassion.

301. The disciples of Gotama are always well awake, and their mind day and night always delights in meditation.

302. It is hard to leave the world (to become a friar), it is hard to enjoy the world; hard is the monastery, painful are the houses; painful it is to dwell with equals (to share everything in common) and the itinerant mendicant is beset with pain. Therefore let no man be an itinerant mendicant and he will not be beset with pain.

303. Whatever place a faithful, virtuous, celebrated, and wealthy man chooses, there he is respected.

304. Good people shine from afar, like the snowy mountains; bad people are not seen, like arrows shot by night.

305. He alone who, without ceasing, practices the duty of sitting alone and sleeping alone, he, subduing himself, will rejoice in the destruction of all desires alone, as if living in a forest.

Chapter XXII The Downward Course

306. He who says what is not, goes to hell; he also who, having done a thing, says I have not done it. After death both are equal, they are men with evil deeds in the next world.

307. Many men whose shoulders are covered with the yellow gown are ill-conditioned and unrestrained; such evil-doers by their evil deeds go to hell.

308. Better it would be to swallow a heated iron ball, like flaring fire, than that a bad unrestrained fellow should live on the charity of the land.

309. Four things does a reckless man gain who covets his neighbor's wife, – a bad reputation, an uncomfortable bed, thirdly, punishment, and lastly, hell.

310. There is bad reputation, and the evil way (to hell), there is the short pleasure of the frightened in the arms of the frightened, and the king imposes heavy punishment; therefore let no man think of his neighbor's wife.

311. As a grass-blade, if badly grasped, cuts the arm, badly-practiced asceticism leads to hell.

312. An act carelessly performed, a broken vow, and hesitating obedience to discipline, all this brings no great reward.

313. If anything is to be done, let a man do it, let him attack it vigorously! A careless pilgrim only scatters the dust of his passions more widely.

314. An evil deed is better left undone, for a man repents of it afterwards; a good deed is better done, for having done it, one does not repent.

315. Like a well-guarded frontier fort, with defenses within and without, so let a man guard himself. Not a moment should escape, for they who allow the right moment to pass, suffer pain when they are in hell.

316. They who are ashamed of what they ought not to be ashamed of, and are not ashamed of what they ought to be ashamed of, such men, embracing false doctrines enter the evil path.

317. They who fear when they ought not to fear, and fear not when they ought to fear, such men, embracing false doctrines, enter the evil path.

318. They who forbid when there is nothing to be forbidden, and forbid not when there is something to be forbidden, such men, embracing false doctrines, enter the evil path.

319. They who know what is forbidden as forbidden, and what is not forbidden as not forbidden, such men, embracing the true doctrine, enter the good path.

Chapter XXIII The Elephant

320. Silently shall I endure abuse as the elephant in battle endures the arrow sent from the bow: for the world is ill-natured.

321. They lead a tamed elephant to battle, the king mounts a tamed elephant; the tamed is the best among men, he who silently endures abuse.

322. Mules are good, if tamed, and noble Sindhu horses, and elephants with large tusks; but he who tames himself is better still.

323. For with these animals does no man reach the untrodden country (Nirvana), where a tamed man goes on a tamed animal, viz. on his own well-tamed self.

324. The elephant called Dhanapalaka, his temples running with sap, and difficult to hold, does not eat a morsel when bound; the elephant longs for the elephant grove.

325. If a man becomes fat and a great eater, if he is sleepy and rolls himself about, that fool, like a hog fed on wash, is born again and again.

326. This mind of mine went formerly wandering about as it liked, as it listed, as it pleased; but I shall now hold it in thoroughly, as the rider who holds the hook holds in the furious elephant.

327. Be not thoughtless, watch your thoughts! Draw yourself out of the evil way, like an elephant sunk in mud.

328. If a man find a prudent companion who walks with him, is wise, and lives soberly, he may walk with him, overcoming all dangers, happy, but considerate.

329. If a man find no prudent companion who walks with him, is wise, and lives soberly, let him walk alone, like a king who has left his conquered country behind,—like an elephant in the forest.

330. It is better to live alone, there is no companionship with a fool; let a man walk alone, let him commit no sin, with few wishes, like an elephant in the forest.

331. If an occasion arises, friends are pleasant; enjoyment is pleasant, whatever be the cause; a good work is pleasant in the hour of death; the giving up of all grief is pleasant.

332. Pleasant in the world is the state of a mother, pleasant the state of a father, pleasant the state of a Samana, pleasant the state of a Brahmana.

333. Pleasant is virtue lasting to old age, pleasant is a faith firmly rooted; pleasant is attainment of intelligence, pleasant is avoiding of sins.

Chapter XXIV Thirst

334. The thirst of a thoughtless man grows like a creeper; he runs from life to life, like a monkey seeking fruit in the forest.

335. Whomsoever this fierce thirst overcomes, full of poison, in this world, his sufferings increase like the abounding Birana grass.

336. He who overcomes this fierce thirst, difficult to be conquered in this world, sufferings fall off from him, like water-drops from a lotus leaf.

337. This salutary word I tell you, 'Do ye, as many as are here assembled, dig up the root of thirst, as he who wants the sweet-scented Usira root must dig up the Birana grass, that Mara (the tempter) may not crush you again and again, as the stream crushes the reeds.'

338. As a tree, even though it has been cut down, is firm so long as its root is safe, and grows again, thus, unless the feeders of thirst are destroyed, the pain (of life) will return again and again.

339. He whose thirst running towards pleasure is exceeding strong in

the thirty-six channels, the waves will carry away that misguided man, viz. his desires which are set on passion.

340. The channels run everywhere, the creeper (of passion) stands sprouting; if you see the creeper springing up, cut its root by means of knowledge.

341. A creature's pleasures are extravagant and luxurious; sunk in lust and looking for pleasure, men undergo (again and again) birth and decay.

342. Men, driven on by thirst, run about like a snared hare; held in fetters and bonds, they undergo pain for a long time, again and again.

343. Men, driven on by thirst, run about like a snared hare; let therefore the mendicant drive out thirst, by striving after passionlessness for himself.

344. He who having got rid of the forest (of lust) (i.e. after having reached Nirvana) gives himself over to forest-life (i.e. to lust), and who, when removed from the forest (i.e. from lust), runs to the forest (i.e. to lust), look at that man! though free, he runs into bondage.

345. Wise people do not call that a strong fetter which is made of iron, wood, or hemp; far stronger is the care for precious stones and rings, for sons and a wife.

346. That fetter wise people call strong which drags down, yields, but is difficult to undo; after having cut this at last, people leave the world, free from cares, and leaving desires and pleasures behind.

347. Those who are slaves to passions, run down with the stream (of desires), as a spider runs down the web which he has made himself; when they have cut this, at last, wise people leave the world free from cares, leaving all affection behind.

348. Give up what is before, give up what is behind, give up what is in the middle, when you go to the other shore of existence; if thy mind is altogether free, thou wilt not again enter into birth and decay.

349. If a man is tossed about by doubts, full of strong passions, and yearning only for what is delightful, his thirst will grow more and more, and he will indeed make his fetters strong.

350. If a man delights in quieting doubts, and, always reflecting, dwells on what is not delightful (the impurity of the body, &c.), he certainly will remove, nay, he will cut the fetter of Mara.

351. He who has reached the consummation, who does not tremble, who is without thirst and without sin, he has broken all the thorns of life: this will be his last body.

352. He who is without thirst and without affection, who

understands the words and their interpretation, who knows the order of letters (those which are before and which are after), he has received his last body, he is called the great sage, the great man.

353. 'I have conquered all, I know all, in all conditions of life I am free from taint; I have left all, and through the destruction of thirst I am free; having learnt myself, whom shall I teach?'

354. The gift of the law exceeds all gifts; the sweetness of the law exceeds all sweetness; the delight in the law exceeds all delights; the extinction of thirst overcomes all pain.

355. Pleasures destroy the foolish, if they look not for the other shore; the foolish by his thirst for pleasures destroys himself, as if he were his own enemy.

356. The fields are damaged by weeds, mankind is damaged by passion: therefore a gift bestowed on the passionless brings great reward.

357. The fields are damaged by weeds, mankind is damaged by hatred: therefore a gift bestowed on those who do not hate brings great reward.

358. The fields are damaged by weeds, mankind is damaged by vanity: therefore a gift bestowed on those who are free from vanity brings great reward.

359. The fields are damaged by weeds, mankind is damaged by lust: therefore a gift bestowed on those who are free from lust brings great reward.

Chapter XXV The Bhikshu (Mendicant)

360. Restraint in the eye is good, good is restraint in the ear, in the nose restraint is good, good is restraint in the tongue.

361. In the body restraint is good, good is restraint in speech, in thought restraint is good, good is restraint in all things. A Bhikshu, restrained in all things, is freed from all pain.

362. He who controls his hand, he who controls his feet, he who controls his speech, he who is well controlled, he who delights inwardly, who is collected, who is solitary and content, him they call Bhikshu.

363. The Bhikshu who controls his mouth, who speaks wisely and calmly, who teaches the meaning and the law, his word is sweet.

364. He who dwells in the law, delights in the law, meditates on the law, follows the law, that Bhikshu will never fall away from the true law.

365. Let him not despise what he has received, nor ever envy others: a mendicant who envies others does not obtain peace of mind.

366. A Bhikshu who, though he receives little, does not despise what he has received, even the gods will praise him, if his life is pure, and if he is not slothful.

367. He who never identifies himself with name and form, and does not grieve over what is no more, he indeed is called a Bhikshu.

368. The Bhikshu who acts with kindness, who is calm in the doctrine of Buddha, will reach the quiet place (Nirvana), cessation of natural desires, and happiness.

369. O Bhikshu, empty this boat! if emptied, it will go quickly; having cut off passion and hatred thou wilt go to Nirvana.

370. Cut off the five (senses), leave the five, rise above the five. A Bhikshu, who has escaped from the five fetters, he is called Oghatinna, 'saved from the flood.'

371. Meditate, O Bhikshu, and be not heedless! Do not direct thy thought to what gives pleasure that you may not for thy heedlessness have to swallow the iron ball (in hell), and that you may not cry out when burning, 'This is pain.'

372. Without knowledge there is no meditation, without meditation

there is no knowledge: he who has knowledge and meditation is near unto Nirvana.

373. A Bhikshu who has entered his empty house, and whose mind is tranquil, feels a more than human delight when he sees the law clearly.

374. As soon as he has considered the origin and destruction of the elements (khandha) of the body, he finds happiness and joy which belong to those who know the immortal (Nirvana).

375. And this is the beginning here for a wise Bhikshu: watchfulness over the senses, contentedness, restraint under the law; keep noble friends whose life is pure, and who are not slothful.

376. Let him live in charity, let him be perfect in his duties; then in the fullness of delight he will make an end of suffering.

377. As the Vassika plant sheds its withered flowers, men should shed passion and hatred, O ye Bhikshus!

378. The Bhikshu whose body and tongue and mind are quieted, who is collected, and has rejected the baits of the world, he is called quiet.

379. Rouse thyself by thyself, examine thyself by thyself, thus self-protected and attentive wilt thou live happily, O Bhikshu!

380. For self is the lord of self, self is the refuge of self; therefore curb

thyself as the merchant curbs a good horse.

381. The Bhikshu, full of delight, who is calm in the doctrine of Buddha will reach the quiet place (Nirvana), cessation of natural desires, and happiness.

382. He who, even as a young Bhikshu, applies himself to the doctrine of Buddha, brightens up this world, like the moon when free from clouds.

Chapter XXVI The Brahmana (Arhat)

383. Stop the stream valiantly, drive away the desires, O Brahmana! When you have understood the destruction of all that was made, you will understand that which was not made.

384. If the Brahmana has reached the other shore in both laws (in restraint and contemplation), all bonds vanish from him who has obtained knowledge.

385. He for whom there is neither this nor that shore, nor both, him, the fearless and unshackled, I call indeed a Brahmana.

386. He who is thoughtful, blameless, settled, dutiful, without passions, and who has attained the highest end, him I call indeed a

Brahmana.

387. The sun is bright by day, the moon shines by night, the warrior is bright in his armor, the Brahmana is bright in his meditation; but Buddha, the Awakened, is bright with splendor day and night.

388. Because a man is rid of evil, therefore he is called Brahmana; because he walks quietly, therefore he is called Samana; because he has sent away his own impurities, therefore he is called Pravragita (Pabbagita, a pilgrim).

389. No one should attack a Brahmana, but no Brahmana (if attacked) should let himself fly at his aggressor! Woe to him who strikes a Brahmana, more woe to him who flies at his aggressor!

390. It advantages a Brahmana not a little if he holds his mind back from the pleasures of life; when all wish to injure has vanished, pain will cease.

391. Him I call indeed a Brahmana who does not offend by body, word, or thought, and is controlled on these three points.

392. After a man has once understood the law as taught by the Well-awakened (Buddha), let him worship it carefully, as the Brahmana worships the sacrificial fire.

393. A man does not become a Brahmana by his platted hair, by his

family, or by birth; in whom there is truth and righteousness, he is blessed, he is a Brahmana.

394. What is the use of platted hair, O fool! what of the raiment of goat-skins? Within thee there is ravening, but the outside you make clean.

395. The man who wears dirty clothing, who is emaciated and covered with veins, who lives alone in the forest, and meditates, him I call indeed a Brahmana.

396. I do not call a man a Brahmana because of his origin or of his mother. He is indeed arrogant, and he is wealthy: but the poor, who is free from all attachments, him I call indeed a Brahmana.

397. Him I call indeed a Brahmana who has cut all fetters, who never trembles, is independent and unshackled.

398. Him I call indeed a Brahmana who has cut the strap and the thong, the chain with all that pertains to it, who has burst the bar, and is awakened.

399. Him I call indeed a Brahmana who, though he has committed no offence, endures reproach, bonds, and stripes, who has endurance for his force, and strength for his army.

400. Him I call indeed a Brahmana who is free from anger, dutiful,

virtuous, without appetite, who is subdued, and has received his last body.

401. Him I call indeed a Brahmana who does not cling to pleasures, like water on a lotus leaf, like a mustard seed on the point of a needle.

402. Him I call indeed a Brahmana who, even here, knows the end of his suffering, has put down his burden, and is unshackled.

403. Him I call indeed a Brahmana whose knowledge is deep, who possesses wisdom, who knows the right way and the wrong, and has attained the highest end.

404. Him I call indeed a Brahmana who keeps aloof both from laymen and from mendicants, who frequents no houses, and has but few desires.

405. Him I call indeed a Brahmana who finds no fault with other beings, whether feeble or strong, and does not kill nor cause slaughter.

406. Him I call indeed a Brahmana who is tolerant with the intolerant, mild with fault-finders, and free from passion among the passionate.

407. Him I call indeed a Brahmana from whom anger and hatred,

pride and envy have dropt like a mustard seed from the point of a needle.

408. Him I call indeed a Brahmana who utters true speech, instructive and free from harshness, so that he offend no one.

409. Him I call indeed a Brahmana who takes nothing in the world that is not given him, be it long or short, small or large, good or bad.

410. Him I call indeed a Brahmana who fosters no desires for this world or for the next, has no inclinations, and is unshackled.

411. Him I call indeed a Brahmana who has no interests, and when he has understood (the truth), does not say How, how? and who has reached the depth of the Immortal.

412. Him I call indeed a Brahmana who in this world is above good and evil, above the bondage of both, free from grief from sin, and from impurity.

413. Him I call indeed a Brahmana who is bright like the moon, pure, serene, undisturbed, and in whom all gaiety is extinct.

414. Him I call indeed a Brahmana who has traversed this miry road, the impassable world and its vanity, who has gone through, and reached the other shore, is thoughtful, guileless, free from doubts, free from attachment, and content.

415. Him I call indeed a Brahmana who in this world, leaving all desires, travels about without a home, and in whom all concupiscence is extinct.

416. Him I call indeed a Brahmana who, leaving all longings, travels about without a home, and in whom all covetousness is extinct.

417. Him I call indeed a Brahmana who, after leaving all bondage to men, has risen above all bondage to the gods, and is free from all and every bondage.

418. Him I call indeed a Brahmana who has left what gives pleasure and what gives pain, who is cold, and free from all germs (of renewed life), the hero who has conquered all the worlds.

419. Him I call indeed a Brahmana who knows the destruction and the return of beings everywhere, who is free from bondage, sojourning (Sugata), and awakened (Buddha).

420. Him I call indeed a Brahmana whose path the gods do not know, nor spirits (Gandharvas), nor men, whose passions are extinct, and who is an Arhat (venerable).

421. Him I call indeed a Brahmana who calls nothing his own, whether it be before, behind, or between, who is poor, and free from the love of the world.

422. Him I call indeed a Brahmana, the manly, the noble, the hero, the great sage, the conqueror, the impassible, the accomplished, the awakened.

423. Him I call indeed a Brahmana who knows his former abodes, who sees heaven and hell, has reached the end of births, is perfect in knowledge, a sage, and whose perfections are all perfect.

Notes:

For a mind to be dissipated (*anavassuta*), is for it to run towards external objects. The mind is on senses and objects.

Mara is the god of death. Mara is the symbol of worldly temptations, and the father of worldly desires. "Desires" (*tamha*) are the cause of birth (*gati*). To defeat desires is to conquest of Mara. Mara's "flower-pointed arrow" is the pleasurable temptations of the physical world through which he slays unsuspecting humans. The oxymoron of an arrow whose point is a flower is meant to illustrate how pleasures do not seem to be dangerous, but in fact are spiritually fatal. The Hindu god of love, Kama, also uses flower-pointed arrows on his victims.

Samsara, (life) is the constant revolution of birth and death which goes on for ever until the knowledge of the doctrine of Buddha enables a man to free himself from samsara, and enters into Nirvana.

The mendicant is a monk who has devoted himself or herself to discovering enlightenment. Mendicant; someone living an ascetic life.

Viveka (understanding) is the "separation," from the world and entering into a life of solitude (*kaya-viveka*). It is also separation from random, undisciplined thoughts (*kitta-viveka*). It is also the separation from elf thus and freedom (*Nirvana*).

T*rividha-dvara* are the three doors of Buddhism: thought, word, deed.

T*amha;* in the army of Mara is a figure representing "thirst" or "desire."

Srmana are among the most famous of Buddha's sayings. They are traditionally thought to be the words the Buddha uttered at the moment he attained to Buddhahood.

"Maker of the tabernacle" refers to the multiple births that form the subject of some verses.

Buddha does not refer to a specific person, but anyone who has arrived at complete knowledge.

Zen Buddhism

Zen is a school of Buddhism, referred to in Chinese as Chán, which means "meditation."

Zen emphasizes direct and personal experience in attaining wisdom as realized in the form of meditation known as zazen. A path to the attainment of awakening is known as the path of enlightenment. As such, it de-emphasizes both theoretical knowledge and the study of religious texts in favor of direct, experiential realization through meditation and dharma practice.

The establishment of Zen is traditionally credited to the South Indian Pallava prince-turned-monk Bodhidharma, who is recorded as having come to China to teach a "special transmission outside scriptures" which "did not stand upon words". The emergence of Zen as a distinct school of Buddhism was first documented in China in the 7th century CE.

Zen is thought to have developed in the combining of various currents in Mahāyāna Buddhist thought and the traditions in China, particularly Taoism and Huáyán Buddhism. From China, Zen subsequently spread southwards to Vietnam and eastwards to Korea and Japan.

Zen teaches that all human beings have the Buddha-nature, or the potential to attain enlightenment, within them, but the Buddha-nature has been clouded by ignorance. To overcome this ignorance, Zen rejects the study of scriptures, religious rites, devotional practices, and good works in favor of meditation leading to a sudden breakthrough of insight and awareness of ultimate reality. Training in the Zen path is usually undertaken by a disciple under the guidance of a master.

Several schools of Zen developed in China in the 9th century. The Rinzai (Chinese, Lin-chi) sect of Zen was introduced to Japan by the Chinese priest Ensai in 1191. Rinzai Buddhism emphasizes the use of koans, paradoxical puzzles or questions that help the practitioner to overcome the normal boundaries of logic. Koans are often accompanied by shouts or slaps from the master, intended to provoke anxiety leading to instant realization of the truth. These teachings influenced the warrior class and led to a Zen influence over the martial arts of archery and swordsmanship.

Soto Buddhism (Chinese, Ts'ao-tung) is another Zen sect that was transmitted from China to Japan. It arrived in Japan in 1227 upon the teacher Dogen's return from China. Soto emphasizes zazen, or sitting meditation, as the means to attain enlightenment. The Soto practitioner is encouraged to clear the mind of all thoughts and concepts, without making any effort towards enlightenment, until enlightenment occurs.

Zen Sayings
THE GATELESS GATE

by Ekai, called Mu-mon

Based of the Transcribed work by Nyogen Senzaki and Paul Reps

1. Joshu's Dog

A monk asked Joshu, a Chinese Zen master: "Does a dog have Buddha-nature or not?"

Joshu answered: "Mu." ["Nothing," "void," or "Nay."]

Mumon's comment: To realize Zen one has to pass through the barrier of the patriarchs. Enlightenment has always come after the path of thinking is blocked. If you do not pass the barrier of the patriarchs or if your thinking path is not blocked, whatever you think, whatever you do, is like a confused ghost. You may ask: What is a barrier of a patriarch? This one word, Mu, is it.

This is the barrier of Zen. If you pass through it you will see Joshu face to face. Then you can work hand in hand with the whole line of patriarchs. Is this not a pleasant thing to do?

If you want to pass this barrier then every bone in your body, every pore in your skin must be filled with this question: What is Mu? And you must carry it day and night.

Do not believe it is the common negative symbol meaning nothing. It is not nothingness, the opposite of existence. If you really want to pass this barrier, you should feel like drinking a hot iron ball that you can neither swallow nor spit out.

Then your previous lesser knowledge disappears. As a fruit ripening in season, your subjectivity and objectivity naturally become one. It is like a dumb man who had a dream. He knows about it but he cannot tell it.

When he enters this condition the shell of his ego is crushed and he can shake the heaven and move the earth. He is like a great warrior with a sharp sword. If a Buddha stands in his way, he will cut him down; if a patriarch offers him any obstacle, he will kill him; and he will be free in his way of birth and death. He can enter any world as if it were his own playground. I will tell you how to do this with this koan:

Simply concentrate your entire energy into Mu, and do not allow any discontinuation. When you enter this Mu and there is no discontinuation, your attainment will be as a candle burning and illuminating the whole universe.

Has a dog Buddha-nature?
This is the most serious question of all.
If you say yes or no,
You lose your own Buddha-nature.

2. Hyakujo's Fox

Once when Hyakujo was delivering Zen lectures an old man was in attendence, unseen by the monks. At the end of each talk, as the monks left so did he. But one day he remained after they had gone, and Hyakujo asked him: "Who are you?"

The old man replied: "I am not a human being, but I was a human being when the Kashapa Buddha preached in this world. Then I was a Zen master living on this mountain. At that time one of my students asked me whether or not the enlightened man is subject to the law of cause and affect. I answered him: 'The enlightened man is not subject to the law of cause and affect.' Because the answer evidenced a clinging to an absolute I became a fox for five hundred rebirths, and I am still a fox. Will you save me from this condition with your Zen words and let me get out of a fox's body? Now may I ask you: Is the enlightened man subject to the law of cause and affect?"

Hyakujo said: "The enlightened man is one with the law of cause and affect."

At the words of Hyakujo the old man was enlightened. "I am set free," he said, paying homage with a deep bow. "I am a fox no more, but now I have to leave my body in my dwelling place behind this mountain. Please perform my funeral as a monk." Then he disappeared.

The next day Hyakujo gave an order through the chief monk to prepare to attend the funeral of a monk. "No one was sick in the infirmary," the monks thought. "What does our teacher mean?"

After dinner Hyakujo led the monks out and around the mountain. With his staff he poked the corpse of an old fox, pointing it out in a cave, and then performed the ceremony of cremation.

That evening Hyakujo gave a talk to the monks and told them this story about the law of cause and affect.

Obaku, upon hearing the story, asked Hyakujo: "I understand that because a person gave a wrong Zen answer a long time ago he became a fox for five hundred rebirths. But now I want to ask: If a modern master is asked many questions and he always gives the right answer, what will become of him?"

Hyakujo said: "You come over here to me and I will tell you."

Obaku went over ot Hyakujo and slapped his teacher's face with his hand, because he knew this was the answer his teacher intended to give him.

Hyakujo clapped his hands and laughed at his discernment. "I thought a Persian had a red beard," he said, "and now I know a Persian who has a red beard."

Mumon's comment: "The enlightened man is not subject." How can this answer make the monk a fox?

"The enlightened man is one with the law of cause and affect." How can this answer set the fox free?

To understand this clearly one has to have just one eye.

Controlled or not controlled?
The same dice shows two faces.
Not controlled or controlled,
Both are a grievous error.

3. Gutei's Finger

Gutei raised his finger whenever he was asked a question about Zen. A boy attendant began to imitate his manner. When anyone asked the boy what his master had preached about, the boy would raise his finger.

Gutei heard about the boy's mischief. He seized him and cut off his finger. The boy cried and ran away. Gutei called to him and stopped him. When the boy turned his head to see Gutei, Gutei raised up his own finger. In that instant the boy was enlightened.

When Gutei was about to pass from this world he gathered his monks around him. "I attained the Zen of my finger," he said, "from my teacher Tenryu, and in my whole life I could not exhaust it." Then he died.

Mumon's comment: Enlightenment, which Gutei and the boy attained, has nothing to do with a finger. If anyone clings to a finger, Tenryu will be so disappointed that he will annihilate Gutei, the boy, and the ones who cling, all together.

Gutei cheapens the teaching of Tenryu,
Emancipating the boy with a knife.
Compared to the Chinese god who pushed aside a mountain with one hand

Old Gutei is a poor imitator.

4. A Beardless Foreigner

Wakuan complained when he saw a picture of bearded Bodhidharma: "Why does that fellow have no beard?"

Mumon's comment: If you want to study Zen, you must study it with your heart. When you attain realization, it must be true realization. You yourself must have the face of the great Bodhidharma to see him. Just one such glimpse will be enough. But if you say you met him, you never saw him at all.

One should not discuss a dream
In front of a simpleton.
Why has Bodhidharma no beard?
What an absurd question!

5. Kyogen Mounts the Tree

Kyogen said: "Zen is like a man hanging in a tree by his teeth over a precipice. His hands do not grasp a branch, his feet do not rest on a limb, and under the tree a person asks him: 'Why did Bodhidharma come to China from India?'

"If the man in the tree does not answer, he fails; and if he does answer, he falls and loses his life. Now what will he do?"

Mumon's comment: In such a predicament the most talented eloquence is of no use. Even if you have memorized all the sutras, you cannot use them. When you can give the right answer, even though your past road was one of death, you open up a new road of life. But if you cannot answer, you should live ages from then and ask the future Buddha, Maitreya.

Kyogen is truly a fool
Spreading that ego-killing poison
That closes his pupils' mouths
And lets their tears stream from their dead eyes.

(Note: Maitreya is the future Buddha and is prophesied in the Sanskrit text, the **Maitreyavyākaraṇa** (The Prophecy of Maitreya), stating that gods, men, and other beings will worship Maitreya; it implies that he is a teacher of trance sadhana:

"will lose their doubts, and the torrents of their cravings will be cut off: free from all misery they will manage to cross the ocean of becoming; and, as a result of Maitreya's teachings, they will lead a holy life. No longer will they regard anything as their own, they will have no possession, no gold or silver, no home, no relatives! But they will lead the holy life of chastity under Maitreya's guidance. They will have torn the net of the passions, they will manage to enter into trances, and theirs will be an abundance of joy and

happiness, for they will lead a holy life under Maitreya's guidance." Trans. in Conze 1959:241)

6. Buddha Twirls a Flower

When Buddha was in Grdhrakuta mountain he twirled a flower in his fingers and held it before his listeners. Every one was silent. Only Maha-Kashapa smiled at this revelation, although he tried to control the lines of his face.

Buddha said: "I have the eye of the true teaching, the heart of Nirvana, the true aspect of formlessness, and the indescribable stride of Dharma. It is not expressed by words, but especially transmitted beyond teaching. This teaching I have given to Maha-Kashapa."

Mumon's comment: Golden-faced Gautama thought he could cheat anyone. He made the good listeners as bad, and sold dog meat under the sign of mutton. And he himself thought it was wonderful. What if all the audience had laughed all together? How could he have transmitted the teaching? On the other hand, what if Maha-Kashapa had not smiled, how could he have transmitted the teaching? If he says that realization can be transmitted, he is like the city slicker that cheats the country bumpkin, because, if he says it cannot be transmitted, why does he approve of Maha-Kashapa?

At the turning of a flower

His disguise was exposed.
No one in heaven or earth can surpass
Maha-Kashapa's wrinkled face.

7. Joshu Washes the Bowl

A monk told Joshu: "I have just entered the monastery. Please teach me."

Joshu asked: "Have you eaten your rice porridge?"

The monk replied: "I have eaten."

Joshu said: "Then you had better wash your bowl."

At that moment the monk was enlightened.

Mumon's comment: Joshu is the man who opens his mouth and shows his heart. I doubt if this monk really saw Joshu's heart. I hope he did not mistake the bell for a pitcher.

It is too clear and so it is hard to see.
A dunce once searched for a fire with a lighted lantern.
Had he known what fire was,
He could have cooked his rice much sooner.

8. Keichu's Wheel

Getsuan said to his students: "The first wheel-maker of China, a man named Keichu, made two wheels of fifty spokes each. Now, suppose you removed the hub uniting the spokes. What would become of the wheel? Had Keichu done this, could he be called the master wheel-maker?"

Mumon's comment: If anyone can answer this question instantly, his eyes will be like a comet and his mind like a flash of lightning.

When the hubless wheel turns,
Master or no master can stop it.
It turns above heaven and below earth,
South, north, east, and west.

9. A Buddha before History

A monk asked Seijo: "I understand that a Buddha who lived before recorded history sat in meditation for ten cycles of existence and could not realize the highest truth, and so could not become fully free. Why was this so?"

Seijo replied: "Your question is self-explanatory."

The monk asked: "Since the Buddha was meditating, why could he not fulfill Buddhahood?"

Seijo said: "He was not a Buddha."

Mumon's comment: I will allow his realization, but I will not admit his understanding. When an ignorant person attains realization he is a saint. When a saint begins to understand he is ignorant.

It is better to realize mind than body.
When mind is realized one need not worry about body.
When mind and body become one
The man is free. Then he desires no praising.

10. Seizei Alone and Poor

A monk named Seizei asked of Sozan: "Seizei is alone and poor. Will you give him support?"

Sozan asked: "Seizei?"

Seizei responded: "Yes, sir."

Sozan said: "You have Zen, which is the best wine in China, and you have already finished three cups, and still you are saying that they did not even wet your lips."

Mumon's comment: Seizei overplayed his hand. Why was it so? Because Sozan had eyes and knew with whom to deal. Even so, I want to ask: At what point did Seizei drink wine?

The poorest man in China,
The bravest man in China,
He barely sustains himself,
Yet wishes to rival the wealthiest.

11. Joshu Examines a Monk in Meditation

Joshu went to a place where a monk had gone to meditate and asked him: "What is, is what?"

The monk raised his fist.

Joshu replied: "Ships cannot remain where the water is too shallow." And he left.

A few days later Joshu went again to visit the monk and asked the same question.

The monk answered the same way.

Joshu said: "Well given, well taken, well killed, well saved." And he bowed to the monk.

Mumon's comment: The raised fist was the same both times. Why is it Joshu did not accept the first but approved the second one? Where is the fault?

Whoever answers this knows that Joshu's tongue has no bone so he can use it freely. Yet perhaps Joshu is wrong. Or, through that monk, he may have discovered his mistake.

If anyone thinks that the one's insight exceeds the other's, he has no eyes.

The light of the eyes is as a comet,
And Zen's activity is as lightning.
The sword that kills the man
Is the sword that saves the man.

12. Zuigan Calls His Own Master

Zuigan called out to himself every day: "Master."

Then he answered himself: "Yes, sir."

And after that he added: "Become sober."

Again he answered: "Yes, sir."

"And after that," he continued, "Do not be deceived (be cheated) by others."

"Yes, sir; yes, sir," he answered.

Mumon's comment: Old Zuigan sells out and buys himself. He is opening a puppet show. He uses one mask to call "Master" and another that answers the master. Another mask says "Sober up" and another says, "Do not be cheated by others." If anyone clings to any of his masks, he is mistaken, yet if he imitates Zuigan, he will make himself fox-like.

Some Zen students do not realize the true man in a mask
Because they recognize ego-soul.
Ego-soul is the seed of birth and death,
And foolish people call it the true man.

13. Tokusan Holds His Bowl

Tokusan went to the dining room from the meditation hall holding his bowl. Seppo was on duty cooking. When he met Tokusan he said: "The dinner drum is not yet beaten. Where are you going with your bowl?"

So Tokusan returned to his room.

Seppo told Ganto about this. Ganto said: "Old Tokusan did not understand ultimate truth."

Tokusan heard of this remark and asked Ganto to come to him. He said, "I have heard you are not approving my Zen." Ganto admitted this indirectly. Tokusan said nothing.

The next day Tokusan delivered an entirely different kind of lecture to the monks. Ganto laughed and clapped his hands, saying: "I see our old man understands ultimate truth indeed. None in China can surpass him."

Mumon's comment: Speaking about ultimate truth, both Ganto and Tokusan did not even dream it. After all, they are dummies.

Whoever understands the first truth
Should understand the ultimate truth.
The last and first,
Are they not the same?

14. Nansen Cuts the Cat in Two

Nansen saw the monks of the eastern and western halls fighting over a cat. He seized the cat and told the monks: "If any of you say a good word, you can save the cat."

No one answered. So Nansen boldly cut the cat in two pieces.

That evening Joshu returned and Nansen told him about this. Joshu removed his sandals and placed them on his head, then walked out.

Nansen said: "If you had been there, you could have saved the cat."

Mumon's comment: Why did Joshu put his sandals on his head? If anyone answers this question, he will understand exactly how Nansen enforced the edict. If not, he should watch his own head.

Had Joshu been there,
He would have enforced the edict oppositely.
Joshu snatches the sword
And Nansen begs for his life.

15. Tozan's Three Blows

Tozan went to Ummon. Ummon asked him where he had come from.

Tozan said: "From Sato village."

Ummon asked: "In what temple did you remain for the summer?"

Tozan replied: "The temple of Hoji, south of the lake."

Ummon asked, "When did you leave there?" wondering how long Tozan would continue with such factual answers.

"The twenty-fifth of August," answered Tozan.

Ummon said: "I should give you three blows with a stick, but today I forgive you."

The next day Tozan bowed to Ummon and asked: "Yesterday you forgave me three blows. I do not know why you thought me wrong."

Ummon, disapproved of Tozan's spiritless responses, and said: "You are good for nothing. You simply wander from one monastery to another."

Before Ummon's words were ended Tozan was enlightened.

Mumon's comment: Ummon fed Tozan good Zen food. If Tozan can digest it, Ummon may add another member to his family.

In the evening Tozan swam around in a sea of good and bad, but at dawn Ummon crushed his nutshell. After all, he wasn't so smart.

Now, I want to ask: Did Tozan deserve the three blows? If you say yes, not only Tozan but every one of you deserves them. If you say no, Ummon is speaking a lie. If you answer this question clearly, you can eat the same food as Tozan.

The lioness teaches her cubs roughly;
The cubs jump and she knocks them down.
When Ummon saw Tozan his first arrow was light;
His second arrow shot deep.

16. Bells and Robes

Ummon asked: "The world is such a wide world, why do you answer a bell and don ceremonial robes?"

Mumon's comment: When one studies Zen one need not follow sound or color or form. Even though some have attained insight when hearing a voice or seeing a color or a form, this is a very common way. It is not true Zen. The real Zen student controls sound, color, form, and actualizes the truth in his everyday life.

Sound comes to the ear, the ear goes to sound. When you blot out sound and sense, what do you understand? While listening with ears one never can understand. To understand intimately one should see sound.

When you understand, you belong to the family;
When you do not understand, you are a stranger.
Those who do not understand belong to the family,
And when they understand they are strangers.

17. The Three Calls of the Emperor's Teacher

Chu, the national teacher - the teacher of the emperor, called to his attendant: "Oshin."

Oshin answered: "Yes."

Chu repeated, to test his pupil: "Oshin."

Oshin repeated: "Yes."

Chu called: "Oshin."

Oshin answered: "Yes."

Chu said: "I ought to apologize to you for all this calling, but really you ought to apologize to me."

Mumon's comment: When old Chu called Oshin three times his tongue was rotting, but when Oshin answered three times his words were brilliant. Chu was getting decrepit and lonesome, and his method of teaching was like holding a cow's head to feed it clover.

Oshin did not trouble to show his Zen either. His satisfied stomach had no desire to feast. When the country is prosperous everyone is indolent; when the home is wealthy the children are spoiled.

Now I want to ask you: Which one should apologize?

When prison stocks are iron and have no place for the head, the prisoner is doubly in trouble.
When there is no place for Zen in the head of our generation, it is in grievous trouble.
If you try to hold up the gate and door of a falling house,
You also will be in trouble.

18. Tozan's Three Pounds

A monk asked Tozan when he was weighing some flax: "What is Buddha?"

Tozan said: "This flax weighs three pounds."

Mumon's comment: Old Tozan's Zen is like a clam. The minute the shell opens you see the whole inside. However, I want to ask you: Do you see the real Tozan?

Three pounds of flax in front of your nose,
Close enough, and mind is still closer.
Whoever talks about affirmation and negation
Lives in the "right and wrong" region.

19. Everyday Life Is the Path

Joshu asked Nansen: "What is the path?"

Nansen said: "Everyday life is the path."

Joshu asked: "Can it be studied?"

Nansen said: "If you try to study (it), you will be far away from it."

Joshu asked: "If I do not study, how can I know it is the path?"

Nansen said: "The path does not belong to the perception world, neither does it belong to the world of no-perception. Thinking is a delusion and non-thinking is senseless. If you want to reach the true path beyond doubt, place yourself in the same freedom as the sky. You name it neither good nor not-good."

At these words Joshu was enlightened.

Mumon's comment: Nansen could melt Joshu's frozen doubts at once when Joshu asked his questions. I doubt though if Joshu reached the point that Nansen did. He needed thirty more years of study.

In spring, hundreds of flowers; in autumn, a harvest moon;
In summer, a refreshing breeze; in winter, snow will accompany you.
If useless things do not hang in your mind,
Any season is a good season for you.

20. The Enlightened Man

Shogen asked: "Why does the enlightened man not stand on his feet and explain himself?" And he also said: "It is not necessary for speech to come from the tongue."

Mumon's comment: Shogen spoke plainly enough, but how many will understand? If anyone comprehends, he should come to my place and test out my big stick. Why, look here, to test real gold you must see it through fire.

If the feet of enlightenment moved, the great ocean would overflow;
If that head bowed, it would look down upon the heavens.
Such a body has no place to rest. . . .
Let another continue this poem.

21. Dried Dung

A monk asked Ummon: "What is Buddha?"

Ummon answered him: "Dried dung."

Mumon's comment: It seems to me Ummon is so poor he cannot distinguish the taste of one food from another, or else he is too busy to write readable letters. Well, he tried to hold his school with dried dung. And his teaching was just as useless.

Lightning flashes,
Sparks shower.
In one blink of your eyes
You have missed seeing.

22. Kashapa's Preaching Sign

Ananda asked Kashapa: "Buddha gave you the golden-woven robe of successorship. What else did he give you?"

Kashapa said: "Ananda."

Ananda answered: "Yes, brother."

Said Kashapa: "Now you can take down my preaching sign and put up your own."

Mumon's comment: If one understands this, he will see the old brotherhood still gathering, but if not, even though he has studied the truth from ages before the Buddhas, he will not attain enlightenment.

The point of the question is dull but the answer is intimate.
How many persons hearing it will open their eyes?
Elder brother calls and younger brother answers,
This spring does not belong to the ordinary season.

23. Do Not Think Good, Do Not Think Not-Good

When he became free the sixth patriarch received from the fifth patriarch the bowl and robe given from the Buddha to his successors, generation after generation.

A monk named E-myo out of envy pursued the patriarch to take this great treasure away from him. The sixth patriarch placed the bowl and robe on a stone in the road and told E-myo: "These objects just symbolize the faith. There is no use fighting over them. If you desire to take them, take them now."

When E-myo went to move the bowl and robe they were as heavy as mountains. He could not budge them. Trembling for shame he said: "I came wanting the teaching, not the material treasures. Please teach me."

The sixth patriarch said: "When you do not think good and when you do not think not-good, what is your true self?"

At these words E-myo was illumined. Perspiration broke out all over his body. He cried and bowed, saying: "You have given me the secret words and meanings. Is there yet a deeper part of the teaching?"

The sixth patriarch replied: "What I have told you is no secret at all.

When you realize your own true self the secret belongs to you."

E-myo said: "I was under the fifth patriarch many years but could not realize my true self until now. Through your teaching I find the source. A person drinks water and knows himself whether it is cold or warm. May I call you my teacher?"

The sixth patriarch replied: "We studied together under the fifth patriarch. Call him your teacher, but just treasure what you have attained."

Mumon's comment: The sixth patriarch certainly was kind in such an emergency. It was as if he removed the skin and seeds from the fruit and then, opening the pupil's mouth, let him eat.

You cannot describe it, you cannot picture it,
You cannot admire it, you cannot sense it.
It is your true self, it has nowhere to hide.
When the world is destroyed, it will not be destroyed.

24. Without Words, Without Silence

A monk asked Fuketsu: "Without speaking, without silence, how can you express the truth?"

Fuketsu observed: "I always remember springtime in southern China.

The birds sing among innumerable kinds of fragrant flowers."

Mumon's comment: Fuketsu used to have lightning Zen. Whenever he had the opportunity, he flashed it. But this time he failed to do so and only borrowed from an old Chinese poem. Never mind Fuketsu's Zen. If you want to express the truth, throw out your words, throw out your silence, and tell me about your own Zen.

Without revealing his own penetration,
He offered another's words, not his to give.
Had he chattered on and on,
Even his listeners would have been embarrassed.

25. Preaching from the Third Seat

In a dream Kyozan went to Maitreya's Pure Land. He recognized himself seated in the third seat in the abode of Maitreya. Someone announced: "Today the one who sits in the third seat will preach."

Kyozan arose and, hitting the gavel, said: "The truth of Mahayana teaching is transcendent, above words and thought. Do you understand?"

Mumon's comment: I want to ask you monks: Did he preach or did he not?

When he opens his mouth he is lost. When he seals his mouth he is lost. If he does not open it, if he does not seal it, he is 108,000 miles from truth.

In the light of day,
Yet in a dream he talks of a dream.
A monster among monsters,
He intended to deceive the whole crowd.

26. Two Monks Roll Up the Screen

Hogen of the Seiryo monastery was about to lecture before dinner when he noticed that the bamboo screen lowered for meditation had not been rolled up. He pointed to it. Two monks arose from the audience and rolled it up.

Hogen, observing the physical moment, said: "The state of the first monk is good, not that of the other."

Mumon's comment: I want to ask you: Which of those two monks gained and which lost? If any of you has one eye, he will see the failure on the teacher's part. However, I am not discussing gain and loss.

When the screen is rolled up the great sky opens,
Yet the sky is not attuned to Zen.
It is best to forget the great sky
And to retire from every wind.

27. It Is Not Mind, It Is Not Buddha, It Is Not Things

A monk asked Nansen: "Is there a teaching no master ever preached before?"

Nansen said: "Yes, there is."

"What is it?" asked the monk.

Nansen replied: "It is not mind, it is not Buddha, it is not things."

Mumon's comment: Old Nansen gave away his treasure-words. He must have been greatly upset.

Nansen was too kind and lost his treasure.
Truly, words have no power.
Even though the mountain becomes the sea,
Words cannot open another's mind.

28. Blow Out the Candle

Tokusan was studying Zen under Ryutan. One night he came to Ryutan and asked many questions. The teacher said: "The night is getting old. Why don't you retire?"

So Tokusan bowed and opened the screen to go out, observing: "It is very dark outside."

Ryutan offered Tokusan a lighted candle to find his way. Just as Tokusan received it, Ryutan blew it out. At that moment the mind of Tokusan was opened.

"What have you attained?" asked Ryutan. "From now on," said Tokusan, "I will not doubt the teacher's words."

The next day Ryutan told the monks at his lecture: "I see one monk among you. His teeth are like the sword tree, his mouth is like the blood bowl. If you hit him hard with a big stick, he will not even so much as look back at you. Someday he will mount the highest peak and carry my teaching there."

On that day, in front of the lecture hall, Tokusan burned to ashes his commentaries on the sutras. He said: "However abstruse the teachings are, in comparison with this enlightenment they are like a single hair to the great sky. However profound the complicated knowledge of the world, compared to this enlightenment it is like one drop of water to the great ocean." Then he left that monastery.

Mumon's comment: When Tokusan was in his own country he was not satisfied with Zen although he had heard about it. He thought: "Those Southern monks say they can teach Dharma outside of the sutras. They are all wrong. I must teach them." So he traveled south. He happened to stop near Ryutan's monastery for refreshments. An old woman who was there asked him: "What are you carrying so heavily?"

Tokusan replied: "This is a commentary I have made on the Diamond Sutra after many years of work."

The old woman said: "I read that sutra which says: 'The past mind cannot be held, the present mind cannot be held, the future mind cannot be held.' You wish some tea and refreshments. Which mind do you propose to use for them?"

Tokusan was as though dumb. Finally he asked the woman: "Do you know of any good teacher around here?"

The old woman referred him to Ryutan, not more than five miles away. So he went to Ryutan in all humility, quite different from when he had started his journey. Ryutan in turn was so kind he forgot his own dignity. It was like pouring muddy water over a drunken man to sober him. After all, it was an unnecessary comedy.

A hundred hearings cannot surpass one seeing,
But after you see the teacher, that one glance cannot surpass a hundred hearings.
His nose was very high
But he was blind after all.

29. Not the Wind, Not the Flag

Two monks were arguing about a flag. One said: "The flag is moving."

The other said: "The wind is moving."

The sixth patriarch happened to be passing by. He told them: "Not the wind, not the flag; mind is moving."

Mumon's comment: The sixth patriarch said: "The wind is not moving, the flag is not moving. Mind is moving." What did he mean? If you understand this intimately, you will see the two monks there trying to buy iron and gaining gold. The sixth patriarch could not bear to see those two dull heads, so he made such a bargain.

Wind, flag, mind moves,

The same understanding.
When the mouth opens
All are wrong.

30. This Mind Is Buddha

Daibai asked Baso: "What is Buddha?"

Baso said: "This mind is Buddha."

Mumon's comment: If anyone fully understands this, he is wearing Buddha's clothing, he is eating Buddha's food, he is speaking Buddha's words, he is behaving as Buddha, he is Buddha. This anecdote, however, has given many a pupil the sickness of formality. If one truly understands, he will wash out his mouth for three days after saying the word Buddha, and he will close his ears and flee after hearing "This mind is Buddha."

Under blue sky, in bright sunlight,
One need not search around.
Asking what Buddha is
Is like hiding loot in one's pocket and declaring oneself innocent.

31. Joshu Investigates

A traveling monk asked an old woman the road to Taizan, a popular temple supposed to give wisdom to the one who worships there. The old woman said: "Go straight ahead." When the monk had walked a few steps, she said to herself: "He also is a common church-goer."

Someone told this incident to Joshu, who said: "Wait until I investigate." The next day he went and asked the same question, and the old woman gave the same answer.

Joshu remarked: "I have investigated that old woman."

Mumon's comment: The old woman understood how war is planned, but she did not know how spies sneak in behind her tent. Old Joshu played the spy's work and turned the tables on her, but he was not an able general. Both had their faults. Now I want to ask you: What was the point of Joshu's investigating the old woman?

When the question is common
The answer is also common.
When the question is sand in a bowl of boiled rice
The answer is a stick in the soft mud.

32. A Philosopher Asks Buddha

A philosopher asked Buddha: "Without words, without the wordless, will you tell me truth?"

The Buddha kept silence.

The philosopher bowed and thanked the Buddha, saying: "With your loving kindness I have cleared away my delusions and entered the true path."

After the philosopher had gone, Ananda asked the Buddha what he had attained.

The Buddha replied: "A good horse runs even at the shadow of the whip."

Mumon's comment: Ananda was the disciple of the Buddha. Even so, his opinion did not surpass that of outsiders. I want to ask you monks: How much difference is there between disciples and outsiders?

To tread the sharp edge of a sword,
To run on smooth-frozen ice,
One needs no footsteps to follow.
Walk over the cliffs with hands free.

33. This Mind Is Not Buddha

A monk asked Baso: "What is Buddha?"

Baso said: "This mind is not Buddha."

Mumon's comment: If anyone understands this, he is a graduate of Zen.

If you meet a fencing-master on the road, you may give him your sword,
If you meet a poet, you may offer him your poem.
When you meet others, say only a part of what you intend.
Never give the whole thing at once.

34. Learning Is Not the Path

Nansen said: "Mind is not Buddha. Learning is not the path."

Mumon's comment: Nansen was getting old and forgot to be ashamed. He spoke out with bad breath and exposed the scandal of his own home. However, there are few who appreciate his kindness.

When the sky is clear the sun appears,

When the earth is parched rain will fall.
He opened his heart fully and spoke out,
But it was useless to talk to pigs and fish.

35. Two Souls

"Seijo, the Chinese girl," observed Goso, "had two souls, one always sick at home and the other in the city, a married woman with two children. Which was the true soul?"

Mumon's comment: When one understands this, he will know it is possible to come out from one shell and enter another, as if one were stopping at a transient lodging house. But if he cannot understand, when his time comes and his four elements separate, he will be just like a crab dipped in boiling water, struggling with many hands and legs. In such a predicament he may say: "Mumon did not tell me where to go!" but it will be too late then.

The moon above the clouds is the same moon,
The mountains and rivers below are all different.
Each is happy in its unity and variety.
This is one, this is two.

36. Meeting a Zen Master on the Road

Goso said: "When you meet a Zen master on the road you cannot talk to him, you cannot face him with silence. What are you going to do?"

Mumon's comment: In such a case, if you can answer him intimately, your realization will be beautiful, but if you cannot, you should look about without seeing anything.

Meeting a Zen master on the road,
Face him neither with words nor silence.
Give him an uppercut
And you will be called one who understands Zen.

37. A Buffalo Passes Through the Enclosure

Goso said: "When a buffalo goes out of his enclosure to the edge of the abyss, his horns and his head and his hoofs all pass through, but why can't the tail also pass?"

Mumon's comment: If anyone can open one eye at this point and say a word of Zen, he is qualified to repay the four gratifications, and, not only that, he can save all sentient beings under him. But if he cannot say such a word of true Zen, he should turn back to his tail.

If the buffalo runs, he will fall into the trench;
If he returns, he will be butchered.
That little tail
Is a very strange thing.

38. An Oak Tree in the Garden

A monk asked Joshu why Bodhidharma came to China.

Joshu said: "An oak tree in the garden."

Mumon's comment: If one sees Joshu's answer clearly, there is no Shakyamuni Buddha before him and no future Buddha after him.

Words cannot describe everything.
The heart's message cannot be delivered in words.
If one receives words literally, he will be lost,
If he tries to explain with words, he will not attain enlightenment in this life.

39. Ummon's Sidetrack

A Zen student told Ummon: "The brilliancy of Buddha illuminates the whole universe."

Before he finished the phrase Ummon asked: "You are reciting another's poem, are you not?"

"Yes," answered the student.

"You are sidetracked," said Ummon.

Afterwards another teacher, Shishin, asked his pupils: "At what point did that student go off the track?"

Mumon's comment: If anyone perceives Ummon's particular skillfulness, he will know at what point the student was off the track, and he will be a teacher of man and deities. If not, he cannot even perceive himself.

When a fish meets the fishhook
If he is too greedy, he will be caught.
When his mouth opens
His life already is lost.

40. Tipping Over a Water Vase

Hyakujo wished to send a monk to open a new monastery. He told his pupils that whoever answered a question most ably would be appointed. Placing a water vase on the ground, he asked: "Who can say what this is without calling its name?"

The chief monk said: "No one can call it a wooden shoe."

Isan, the cooking monk, tipped over the vase with his foot and went out.

Hyakujo smiled and said: "The chief monk loses." And Isan became the master of the new monastery.

Mumon's comment: Isan was brave enough, but he could not escape Hyakujo's trick. After all, he gave up a light job and took a heavy one. Why, can't you see, he took off his comfortable hat and placed himself in iron stocks.

Giving up cooking utensils,
Defeating the chatterbox,
Though his teacher sets a barrier for him
His feet will tip over everything, even the Buddha.

41. Bodhidharma Pacifies the Mind

Bodhidharma sits facing the wall. His future successor stands in the snow and presents his severed arm to Bodhidharma. He cries: "My mind is not pacified. Master, pacify my mind."

Bodhidharma says: "If you bring me that mind, I will pacify it for you."

The successor says: "When I search my mind I cannot hold it."

Bodhidharma says: "Then your mind is pacified already."

Mumon's comment: That broken-toothed old Hindu, Bodhidharma, came thousands of miles over the sea from India to China as if he had something wonderful. He is like raising waves without wind. After he remained years in China he had only one disciple and that one lost his arm and was deformed. Alas, ever since he has had brainless disciples.

Why did Bodhidharma come to China?
For years monks have discussed this.
All the troubles that have followed since
Came from that teacher and disciple.

42. The Girl Comes Out from Meditation

In the time of Buddha Shakyamuni, Manjusri went to the assemblage of the Buddhas. When he arrived there, the conference was over and each Buddha had returned to his own Buddha-land. Only one girl was yet unmoved in deep meditation.

Manjusri asked Buddha Shakyamuni how it was possible for this girl to reach this state, one which even he could not attain. "Bring her out from Samadhi and ask her yourself," said the Buddha.

Manjusri walked around the girl three times and snapped his fingers. She still remained in meditation. So by his miracle power he transported her to a high heaven and tried his best to call her, but in vain.

Buddha Shakyamuni said: "Even a hundred thousand Manjusris could not disturb her, but below this place, past twelve hundred million countries, is a Bodhisattva, Mo-myo, seed of delusion. If he comes here, she will awaken."

No sooner had the Buddha spoken than that Bodhisattva sprang up from the earth and bowed and paid homage to the Buddha. Buddha directed him to arouse the girl. The Bodhisattva went in front of the girl and snapped his fingers, and in that instant the girl came out from her deep meditation.

Mumon's comment: Old Shakyamuni set a very poor stage. I want to ask you monks: If Manjusri, who is supposed to have been the teacher of seven Buddhas, could not bring this girl out of meditation, how then could a Bodhisattva who was a mere beginner?

If you understand this intimately, you yourself can enter the great meditation while you are living in the world of delusion.

One could not awaken her, the other could.
Neither are good actors.
One wears the mask of god, one a devil's mask.
Had both failed, the drama still would be a comedy.

43. Shuzan's Short Staff

Shuzan held out his short staff and said: "If you call this a short staff, you oppose its reality. If you do not call it a short staff, you ignore the fact. Now what do you wish to call this?"

Mumon's comment: If you call this a short staff, you oppose its reality. If you do not call it a short staff, you ignore the fact. It cannot be expressed with words and it cannot be expressed without words.

Now say quickly what it is.

Holding out the short staff,
He gave an order of life or death.
Positive and negative interwoven,
Even Buddhas and patriarchs cannot escape this attack.

44. Basho's Staff

Basho said to his disciple: "When you have a staff, I will give it to you. If you have no staff, I will take it away from you."

Mumon's comment: When there is no bridge over the creek the staff will help me. When I return home on a moonless night the staff will accompany me. But if you call this a staff, you will enter hell like an arrow.

With this staff in my hand
I can measure the depths and shallows of the world.
The staff supports the heavens and makes firm the earth.
Everywhere it goes the true teaching will be spread.

45. Who Is He?

Hoen said: "The past and future Buddhas, both are his servants. Who is he?"

Mumon's comment: If you realize clearly who he is, it is as if you met your own father on a busy street. There is no need to ask anyone whether or not your recognition is true.

Do not fight with another's bow and arrow.
Do not ride another's horse.
Do not discuss another's faults.
Do not interfere with another's work.

46. Proceed from the Top of the Pole

Sekiso asked: "How can you proceed on from the top of a hundred-foot pole?" Another Zen teacher said: "One who sits on the top of a hundred-foot pole has attained a certain height but still is not handling Zen freely. He should proceed on from there and appear with his whole body in the ten parts of the world."

Mumon's comment: One can continue his steps or turn his body freely about on the top of the pole. In either case he should be respected. I want to ask you monks, however: How will you proceed from the top of that pole? Look out!

The man who lacks the third eye of insight
Will cling to the measure of the hundred feet.
Such a man will jump from there and kill himself,
Like a blind man misleading other blind men.

47. Three Gates of Tosotsu

Tosotsu built three barriers and made the monks pass through them. The first barrier is studying Zen. In studying Zen the aim is to see one's own true nature. Now where is your true nature?

Secondly, when one realizes his own true nature he will be free from birth and death. Now when you shut the light from your eyes and become a corpse, how can you free yourself?

Thirdly, if you free yourself from birth and death, you should know where you are. Now your body separates into the four elements. Where are you?

Mumon's comment: Whoever can pass these three barriers will be a master wherever he stands. Whatever happens about him he will turn into Zen.

Otherwise he will be living on poor food and not even enough of that to satisfy himself.

An instant realization sees endless time.
Endless time is as one moment.
When one comprehends the endless moment
He realizes the person who is seeing it.

48. One Road of Kembo

A Zen pupil asked Kembo: "All Buddhas of the ten parts of the universe enter the one road of Nirvana. Where does that road begin?"

Kembo, raising his walking stick and drawing the figure one in the air, said: "Here it is."

This pupil went to Ummon and asked the same question. Ummon, who happened to have a fan in his hand, said: "This fan will reach to the thirty-third heaven and hit the nose of the presiding deity there. It is like the Dragon Carp of the Eastern Sea tipping over the rain-cloud with his tail."

Mumon's comment: One teacher enters the deep sea and scratches the earth and raises dust. The other goes to the mountain top and raises waves that almost touch heaven. One holds, the other gives out. Each supports the profound teaching with a single hand. Kembo and Ummon are like two riders neither of whom can surpass the other. It is very difficult to find the perfect man. Frankly, neither of them know where the road starts.

Before the first step is taken the goal is reached.
Before the tongue is moved the speech is finished.
More than brilliant intuition is needed
To find the origin of the right road.

49. Amban's Addition

Amban, a layman Zen student, said: "Mu-mon has just published forty-eight koans and called the book *Gateless Gate*. He criticizes the old patriarchs' words and actions. I think he is very mischievous. He is like an old doughnut seller trying to catch a passerby to force his doughnuts down his mouth. The customer can neither swallow nor spit out the doughnuts, and this causes suffering. Mu-mon has annoyed everyone enough, so I think I shall add one more as a bargain. I wonder if he himself can eat this bargain. If he can, and digest it well, it will be fine, but if not, we will have to put it back into the frying pan with his forty-eight also and cook them again. Mu-mon, you eat first, before someone else does:

"Buddha, according to a sutra, once said: 'Stop, stop. Do not speak. The ultimate truth is not even to think.'"

Amban's comment: Where did that so-called teaching come from? How is it that one could not even think it? Suppose someone spoke about it then what became of it? Buddha himself was a great chatterbox and in this sutra spoke contrarily. Because of this, persons like Mu-mon appear afterwards in China and make useless doughnuts, annoying people. What shall we do after all? I will show you.

Then Amban put his palms together, folded his hands, and said: "Stop, stop. Do not speak. The ultimate truth is not even to think. And now I will make a little circle on the sutra with my finger and add that five thousand other sutras and Vimalakirti's gateless gate all are here!"

If anyone tells you fire is light,
Pay no attention.
When two thieves meet they need no introduction:
They recognize each other without question.

One Reality only –

How deep and far-reaching!

The ten thousand things –

How confusingly manifold!

The true and the conventional are indeed intermingling,

But they are essentially of the same substance.

The wise and the unenlightened are indeed distinguishable,

But in the Way they are united as one.

Do you desire to find its limits?

How broadly expanding! It is limitless!

How vaguely it vanishes away! Its ends are never reached!

It originates in beginningless time, it terminates in endless time.

THE UPANISHADS

THE UPANISHADS

History

The Term "Upanishad" literally means, "to sit close around." It was the term for a teaching session. Thus, in time the word came to point more toward the secret teaching than the sessions themselves. The word was first used to refer to a set of short statements that conveyed the essence of a doctrine. Later the term grew in scope to refer to entire texts of esoteric knowledge. The tradition or liturgy for conveyance came to be called the Vedas."

The Vedas is a Sanskrit word meaning "knowledge." It is a large body of texts originating in ancient India. Vedas form the oldest layer of literature and the oldest Hindu text.

The texts, called Upanishads, came to be regarded as the teachings forming the concluding section of the Vedic corpus. Though today they are in the public domain, they were originally secret teachings, as the origin of the word suggests.

The earliest Upanishads were pre-Buddhist and were probably written around 800-600 BCE. Only 13 of the Upanishads are regarded as "classical" and were written in this period, however Upanishads continued to be composed long into the Common Era. The traditional teachings include 108, but there are now a total of about 200. Composition occurred in three periods of time. The first and most ancient Upanishads were written before sixth century BCE. They include:

Brhadaranyaka

Chandogya

Taittiraya

Aitareya

Kausataki

Kena

Upanishads containing a more rhythmic structure, called the Metrical, were written around sixth-fifth centuries BCE. They include:

Katha

Avetaavatara

Mundaka

Mahanarayana

The last period to be included in was in now called the "traditional set" or "Later Prose" were composed in the late fifth to early fourth centuries BCE and include:

Praana

Maitri

Mandukya

The Upanishads are brilliant flashes of insight wrapped in words. They are in no particular order and there is no "curriculum" espoused within the sequence. As years pass and doctrine changes, some were thought to convey obsolete teachings and some carried a fresher approach, but all verses were kept in the teachings.

The Main teachings of the Upanishads is a search for an immutable truth and a deeper, permanent reality for the universe and one's own state of being. Breath and mind are used and harnessed to achieve the quest. The quest is to "drill down" into the core of the person to find that thing that existed for all time. The person is divided into layers or Sheaths. The outermost sheath is the sheath of food, which is the physical body. Then we ascend deeper, into the sheath of breath, the sheath of mind, the sheath of intelligence, and finally to the sheath of bliss, which is called the atman, or the "self".

The purpose or goal of self or atman is to become one with the Brahman, which is the ultimate principle of the entire universe and is "Sat", or "Pure Being."

Each individual attains freedom (moksha) through identifying himself with Brahman. Indeed, it is not enough to identify oneself with the Brahman but Upanishads teach that one realizes that one is Brahman. Atman becomes Brahman and self becomes universal. At this point the distinction between the self and the universal consciousness ceases. This idea is expressed in the famous saying,

"Tat tvam asi – "That thou art." Although some may regard this teaching as the one and only goal of the Upanishads, there are equally important doctrines as well.

Since deeper philosophies lack a clear language and roadmap, seeing that it is an entirely internal process, the relationship of Brahman to the Universe can seem confusing. Some Upanishad passages present Brahman as totally separate from the rational or physical world, and thus use the term "unknowable." Other passages indicate Brahman is the source of the universe and its creator, as a candle emits a web of light.

As the atman becomes Brahman all duality collapses into a singularity. Since knowledge or descriptions are based in comparisons and dualities the Brahman is said to be unknowable and not discribable. Since no attributes remain to describe it, Brahman is spoken of in negative terms: neti, neti – "not thus, not thus." Although pictures depict Brahman, it is not a god as we would conceive it to be, but rather a force, a state, a condition, and a power.

It is as if one must acquire knowledge of all that Brahman is not in order to discover the truth of what it is and achieve liberation. The nature of Moksha, or liberation is experiencing the reality of Brahman and is the end of suffering and rebirth. This state, like Brahman itself, cannot be described but is called, "bliss."

A liberated person, or javanmukta, continues to live a human life, subject to the ills of the world, but is completely one with Brahman, and no longer subject to karma. After liberation, a person creates no new karma, but remains in samsara until all past karma has been purged. After this he escapes rebirth.

The Upanishads

Translated and Commentated

by

Swami Paramananda

From the Original Sanskrit Text

This volume is reverently dedicated to all seekers of truth and lovers of wisdom

Preface

The translator's idea of rendering the Upanishads into clear simple English, accessible to Occidental readers, had its origin in a visit paid to a Boston friend in 1909. The gentleman, then battling with a fatal malady, took from his library shelf a translation of the Upanishads and, opening it, expressed deep regret that the obscure and unfamiliar form shut from him what he felt to be profound and vital teaching.

The desire to unlock the closed doors of this ancient treasure house, awakened at that time, led to a series of classes on the Upanishads at The Vedanta Centre of Boston during its early days in St. Botolph Street. The translation and commentary then given were transcribed and, after studious revision, were published in the Centre's monthly magazine, "The Message of the East," in 1913 and 1914.. Still further revision has brought it to its present form.

So far as was consistent with a faithful rendering of the Sanskrit text, the Swami throughout his translation has sought to eliminate all that might seem obscure and confusing to the modern mind. While retaining in remarkable measure the rhythm and archaic force of the lines, he has tried not to sacrifice directness and simplicity of style. Where he has been obliged to use the Sanskrit term for lack of an exact English equivalent, he has invariably interpreted it by a familiar English word in brackets; and everything has been done to remove the sense of strangeness in order that the Occidental reader may not feel himself an alien in the new regions of thought opened to him.

Even more has the Swami striven to keep the letter subordinate to the spirit. Any Scripture is only secondarily an historical document. To treat it as an object of mere intellectual curiosity is to cheat the world of its deeper message. If mankind is to derive the highest benefit from a study of it, its appeal must be primarily to the spiritual consciousness; and one of the salient merits of the present translation lies in this, that the translator approaches his task not only with the grave concern of the careful scholar, but also with the profound reverence and fervor of the true devotee.

Editor
Boston, March, 1919

Contents

Introduction

The Upanishads represent the loftiest heights of ancient Indo-Aryan thought and culture. They form the wisdom portion or Gnana-Kanda of the Vedas, as contrasted with the Karma-Kanda or sacrificial portion. In each of the four great Vedas--known as Rik, Yajur, Sama and Atharva--there is a large portion which deals predominantly with rituals and ceremonials, and which has for its aim to show man how by the path of right action he may prepare himself for higher attainment. Following this in each Veda is another portion called the Upanishad, which deals wholly with the essentials of philosophic discrimination and ultimate spiritual vision. For this reason the Upanishads are known as the Vedanta, that is, the end or final goal of wisdom (Veda, wisdom; anta, end).

The name Upanishad has been variously interpreted. Many claim that it is a compound Sanskrit word Upa-ni-shad, signifying "sitting at the feet or in the presence of a teacher"; while according to other authorities it means "to shatter" or "to destroy" the fetters of ignorance. Whatever may have been the technical reason for selecting this name, it was chosen undoubtedly to give a picture of aspiring seekers "approaching" some wise Seer in the seclusion of an Himalayan forest, in order to learn of him the profoundest truths regarding the cosmic universe and God. Because these teachings were usually given in the stillness of some distant retreat, where the noises of the world could not disturb the tranquillity of the contemplative life, they are known also as Aranyakas, Forest Books. Another reason for this name may be found in the fact that they were intended especially for the Vanaprasthas (those who, having fulfilled all their duties in the world, had retired to the forest to devote themselves to spiritual study).

The form which the teaching naturally assumed was that of dialogue, a form later adopted by Plato and other Greek philosophers. As nothing was written and all instruction was transmitted orally, the Upanishads are called Srutis, "what is heard." The term was also used in the sense of revealed, the Upanishads being regarded as direct revelations of God; while the Smritis, minor Scriptures "recorded through memory," were traditional works of purely human origin. It is a significant fact that nowhere in the Upanishads is mention made of any author or recorder.

No date for the origin of the Upanishads can be fixed, because the written text does not limit their antiquity. The word Sruti makes that clear to us. The teaching probably existed ages before it was set down in any written form. The text itself bears evidence of this, because not infrequently in a dialogue between teacher and disciple the teacher quotes from earlier Scriptures now unknown to us. As Professor Max Muller states in his lectures on the Vedanta Philosophy: "One feels certain that behind all these lightning-flashes of religious and philosophic thought there is a distant past, a dark background of which we shall never know the beginning." Some scholars place the Vedic period as far back as 4000 or 5000 B.C.; others from 2000 to 1400 B.C. But even the most conservative admit that it antedates, by several centuries at least, the Buddhistic period which begins in the sixth century B.C.

The value of the Upanishads, however, does not rest upon their antiquity, but upon the vital message they contain for all times and all peoples. There is nothing peculiarly racial or local in them. The ennobling lessons of these Scriptures are as practical for the modern world as they were for the Indo-Aryans of the earliest Vedic age. Their teachings are summed up in two Maha-Vakyam or "great sayings":--Tat twam asi (That thou art) and Aham Brahmasmi (I am Brahman). This oneness of Soul and God lies at the very root of all Vedic thought, and it is this dominant ideal of the unity of all life and the oneness of Truth which makes the study of the Upanishads especially beneficial at the present moment.

One of the most eminent of European Orientalists writes: "If we fix our attention upon it (this fundamental dogma of the Vedanta system) in its philosophical simplicity as the identity of God and the Soul, the Brahman and the Atman, it will be found to possess a significance reaching far beyond the Upanishads, their time and country; nay, we claim for it an inestimable value for the whole race of mankind. .

Whatever new and unwonted paths the philosophy of the future may strike out, this principle will remain permanently unshaken and from it no deviation can possibly take place. If ever a general solution is reached of the great riddle . . . the key can only be found where alone the secret of nature lies open to us from within, that is to say, in our innermost self. It was here that for the first time the original thinkers of the Upanishads, to their immortal honor, found it...."

The first introduction of the Upanishads to the Western world was through a translation into Persian made in the seventeenth century. More than a century later the distinguished French scholar, Anquetil Duperron, brought a copy of the manuscript from Persia to France and translated it into French and Latin. Publishing only the Latin text. Despite the distortions which must have resulted from transmission through two alien languages, the light of the thought still shone with such brightness that it drew from Schopenhauer the fervent words: "How entirely does the Oupnekhat (Upanishad) breathe throughout the holy spirit of the Vedas! How is every one, who by a diligent study of its Persian Latin has become familiar with that incomparable book, stirred by that spirit to the very depth of his Soul! From every sentence deep, original and sublime thoughts arise, and the whole is pervaded by a high and holy and earnest spirit." Again he says: "The access to (the Vedas) by means of the Upanishads is in my eyes the greatest privilege which this still young century (1818) may claim before all previous centuries." This testimony is borne out by the thoughtful American scholar, Thoreau, who writes: "What extracts from the Vedas I have read fall on me like the light of a higher and purer luminary which describes a loftier course through a purer stratum free from particulars, simple, universal."

The first English translation was made by a learned Hindu, Raja Ram Mohun Roy (1775-1833). Since that time there have been various European translations--French, German, Italian and English. But a mere translation, however accurate and sympathetic, is not sufficient to make the Upanishads accessible to the Occidental mind. Professor Max Muller after a lifetime of arduous labor in this field frankly confesses: "Modern words are round, ancient words are square, and we may as well hope to solve the quadrature of the circle, as to express adequately the ancient thought of the Vedas in modern English."

Without a commentary it is practically impossible to understand either the spirit or the meaning of the Upanishads. They were never designed as popular Scriptures. They grew up essentially as text books of God-knowledge and Self-knowledge, and like all text books they need interpretation. Being transmitted orally from teacher to disciple, the style was necessarily extremely condensed and in the form of aphorisms. The language also was often metaphorical and obscure. Yet if one has the perseverance to penetrate beneath these mere surface difficulties, one is repaid a hundredfold; for these ancient Sacred Books contain the most precious gems of spiritual thought.

Every Upanishad begins with a Peace Chant (Shanti-patha) to create the proper atmosphere of purity and serenity. To study about God the whole nature must be prepared, so unitedly and with loving hearts teacher and disciples prayed to the Supreme Being for His grace and protection. It is not possible to comprehend the subtle problems of life unless the thought is tranquil and the energy concentrated. Until our mind is withdrawn from the varied distractions and agitations of worldly affairs, we cannot enter into the spirit of higher religious study. No study is of avail so long as our inner being is not attuned. We must hold a peaceful attitude towards all living things; and if it is lacking, we must strive fervently to cultivate it through suggestion by chanting or repeating some holy text. The same lesson is taught by Jesus the Christ when He says: "If thou bring thy gift to the altar and there rememberest that thy brother hath aught against thee; leave there thy gift before the altar and go thy way; first be reconciled to thy brother, and then come and offer thy gift."

Bearing this lofty ideal of peace in our minds, let us try to make our hearts free from prejudice, doubt and intolerance, so that from these sacred writings we may draw in abundance inspiration, love and wisdom.

Paramananda

Isa-Upanishad

This Upanishad desires its title from the opening words Isa-vasya, "God-covered." The use of Isa (Lord)--a more personal name of the Supreme Being than Brahman, Atman or Self, the names usually found in the Upanishads--constitutes one of its peculiarities. It forms the closing chapter of the Yajur-Veda, known as Shukla (White).

Oneness of the Soul and God, and the value of both faith and works as means of ultimate attainment are the leading themes of this Upanishad. The general teaching of the Upanishads is that works alone, even the highest, can bring only temporary happiness and must inevitably bind a man unless through them he gains knowledge of his real Self. To help him acquire this knowledge is the aim of this and all Upanishads.

Isa-Upanishad

Peace Chant

OM! That (the Invisible-Absolute) is whole; whole is this (the visible phenomenal); from the Invisible Whole comes forth the visible whole. Though the visible whole has come out from that Invisible Whole, yet the Whole remains unaltered.

OM! PEACE! PEACE! PEACE!

The indefinite term "That" is used in the Upanishads to designate the Invisible-Absolute, because no word or name can fully define It. A finite object, like a table or a tree, can be defined; but God, who is infinite and unbounded, cannot be expressed by finite language. Therefore the Rishis or Divine Seers, desirous not to limit the Unlimited, chose the indefinite term "That" to designate the Absolute.

In the light of true wisdom the phenomenal and the Absolute are inseparable. All existence is in the Absolute; and whatever exists, must exist in It; hence all manifestation is merely a modification of the One Supreme Whole, and neither increases nor diminishes It. The Whole therefore remains unaltered.

I

All this, whatsoever exists in the universe, should be covered by the Lord. Having renounced (the unreal), enjoy (the Real). Do not covet the wealth of any man.

We cover all things with the Lord by perceiving the Divine Presence everywhere. When the consciousness is firmly fixed in God, the conception of diversity naturally drops away; because the One Cosmic Existence shines through all things. As we gain the light of wisdom, we cease to cling to the unrealities of this world and we find all our joy in the realm of Reality.

The word "enjoy" is also interpreted by the great commentator Sankaracharya as "protect," because knowledge of our true Self is the greatest protector and sustainer. If we do not have this knowledge, we cannot be happy; because nothing on this external plane of phenomena is permanent or dependable. He who is rich in the knowledge of the Self does not covet external power or possession.

II

If one should desire to live in this world a hundred years, one should live performing Karma (righteous deeds). Thus thou mayest live; there is no other way. By doing this, Karma (the fruits of thy actions) will not defile thee.

If a man still clings to long life and earthly possessions, and is therefore unable to follow the path of Self-knowledge (Gnana-Nishta) as prescribed in the first Mantram (text), then he may follow the path of right action (Karma-Nishta). Karma here means actions performed without selfish motive, for the sake of the Lord alone. When a man performs actions clinging blindly to his lower desires, then his actions bind him to the plane of ignorance or the plane of birth and death; but when the same actions are performed with surrender to God, they purify and liberate him.

III

After leaving their bodies, they who have killed the Self go to the worlds of the Asuras, covered with blinding ignorance.

The idea of rising to bright regions as a reward for well-doers, and of falling into realms of darkness as a punishment for evil-doers is common to all great religions. But Vedanta claims that this condition of heaven and hell is only temporary; because our actions, being finite, can produce only a finite result.

What does it mean "to kill the Self?" How can the immortal Soul ever be destroyed? It cannot be destroyed, it can only be obscured. Those who hold themselves under the sway of ignorance, who serve the flesh and neglect the Atman or the real Self, are not able to perceive the effulgent and indestructible nature of their Soul; hence they fall into the realm where the Soul light does not shine. Here the Upanishad shows that the only hell is absence of knowledge. As long as man is overpowered by the darkness of ignorance, he is the slave of Nature and must accept whatever comes as the fruit of his thoughts and deeds. When he strays into the path of unreality, the Sages declare that he destroys himself; because he who clings to the perishable body and regards it as his true Self must experience death many times.

IV

That One, though motionless, is swifter than the mind. The senses can never overtake It, for It ever goes before. Though immovable, It travels faster than those who run. By It the all-pervading air sustains all living beings.

This verse explains the character of the Atman or Self. A finite object can be taken from one place and put in another, but it can only occupy one space at a time. The Atman, however, is present everywhere; hence, though one may run with the greatest swiftness to overtake It, already It is there before him.

Even the all-pervading air must be supported by this Self, since It is infinite; and as nothing can live without breathing air, all living things must draw their life from the Cosmic Self.

V

It moves and It moves not. It is far and also It is near. It is within and also It is without all this.

It is near to those who have the power to understand It, for It dwells in the heart of every one; but It seems far to those whose mind is covered by the clouds of sensuality and self-delusion. It is within, because It is the innermost Soul of all creatures; and It is without as the essence of the whole external universe, infilling it like the all-pervading ether.

VI

He who sees all beings in the Self and the Self in all beings, he never turns away from It (the Self).

VII

He who perceives all beings as the Self' for him how can there be delusion or grief, when he sees this oneness (everywhere) ?

He who perceives the Self everywhere never shrinks from anything, because through his higher consciousness he feels united with all life. When a man sees God in all beings and all beings in God, and also God dwelling in his own Soul, how can he hate any living thing? Grief and delusion rest upon a belief in diversity, which leads to competition and all forms of selfishness. With the realization of oneness, the sense of diversity vanishes and the cause of misery is removed.

VIII

He (the Self) is all-encircling, resplendent, bodiless, spotless, without sinews, pure, untouched by sin, all-seeing, all-knowing, transcendent, self-existent; He has disposed all things duly for eternal years.

This text defines the real nature of the Self. When our mind is cleansed from the dross of matter, then alone can we behold the vast, radiant, subtle, ever-pure and spotless Self, the true basis of our existence.

IX

They enter into blind darkness who worship Avidya (ignorance and delusion); they fall, as it were, into greater darkness who worship Vidya (knowledge).

X

By Vidya one end is attained; by Avidya, another. Thus we have heard from the wise men who taught this.

XI

He who knows at the same time both Vidya and Avidya, crosses over death by Avidya and attains immortality through Vidya.

Those who follow or "worship" the path of selfishness and pleasure (Avidya), without knowing anything higher, necessarily fall into darkness; but those who worship or cherish Vidya (knowledge) for mere intellectual pride and satisfaction, fall into greater darkness, because the opportunity which they misuse is greater.

In the subsequent verses Vidya and Avidya are used in something the same sense as "faith" and "works" in the Christian Bible; neither alone can lead to the ultimate goal, but when taken together they carry one to the Highest. Work done with unselfish motive purifies the mind and enables man to perceive his undying nature. From this he gains inevitably a knowledge of God, because the Soul and God are one and inseparable; and when he knows himself to be one with the Supreme and Indestructible Whole, he realizes his immortality.

XII

They fall into blind darkness who worship the Unmanifested and they fall into greater darkness who worship the manifested.

XIII

By the worship of the Unmanifested one end is attained; by the worship of the manifested, another. Thus we have heard from the wise men who taught us this.

XIV

He who knows at the same time both the Unmanifested (the cause of manifestation) and the destructible or manifested, he crosses over death through knowledge of the destructible and attains immortality through knowledge of the First Cause (Unmanifested).

This particular Upanishad deals chiefly with the Invisible Cause and the visible manifestation, and the whole trend of its teaching is to show that they are one and the same, one being the outcome of the other hence no perfect knowledge is possible without simultaneous comprehension of both. The wise men declare that he who worships in a one-sided way, whether the visible or the invisible, does not reach the highest goal. Only he who has a co-ordinated understanding of both the visible and the invisible, of matter and spirit, of activity and that which is behind activity, conquers Nature and thus overcomes death. By work, by making the mind steady and by following the prescribed rules given in the Scriptures, a man gains wisdom. By the light of that wisdom he is able to perceive the Invisible Cause in all visible forms.
Therefore the wise man sees Him in every manifested form. They who have a true conception of God are never separated from Him. They exist in Him and He in them.

XV

The face of Truth is hidden by a golden disk. O Pushan (Effulgent Being)! Uncover (Thy face) that I, the worshipper of Truth, may behold Thee.

XVI

O Pushan! O Sun, sole traveller of the heavens, controller of all, son of Prajapati, withdraw Thy rays and gather up Thy burning effulgence. Now through Thy Grace I behold Thy blessed and glorious form. The Purusha (Effulgent Being) who dwells within Thee, I am He.

Here the sun, who is the giver of all light, is used as the symbol of the Infinite, giver of all wisdom. The seeker after Truth prays to the Effulgent One to control His dazzling rays, that his eyes, no longer blinded by them, may behold the Truth. Having perceived It, he proclaims: "Now I see that that Effulgent Being and I are one and the same, and my delusion is destroyed." By the light of Truth he is able to discriminate between the real and the unreal, and the knowledge thus gained convinces him that he is one with the Supreme; that there is no difference between himself and the Supreme Truth; or as

Christ said, "I and my Father are one."

XVII

May my life-breath go to the all-pervading and immortal Prana, and let this body be burned to ashes. Om! O mind, remember thy deeds! O mind, remember, remember thy deeds! Remember!

Seek not fleeting results as the reward of thy actions, O mind! Strive only for the Imperishable. This Mantram or text is often chanted at the hour of death to remind one of the perishable nature of the body and the eternal nature of the Soul. When the clear vision of the distinction between the mortal body and the immortal Soul dawns in the heart, then all craving for physical pleasure or material possession drops away; and one can say, let the body be burned to ashes that the Soul may attain its freedom; for death is nothing more than the casting-off of a worn-out garment.

XVIII

O Agni (Bright Being)! Lead us to blessedness by the good path. O Lord! Thou knowest all our deeds, remove all evil and delusion from us. To Thee we offer our prostrations and supplications again and again.

Here ends this Upanishad

This Upanishad is called Isa-Vasya-Upanishad, that which gives Brahma-Vidya or knowledge of the All-pervading Deity. The dominant thought running through it is that we cannot enjoy life or realize true happiness unless we consciously "cover" all with the Omnipresent Lord. If we are not fully conscious of that which sustains our life, how can we live wisely and perform our duties? Whatever we see, movable or immovable, good or bad, it is all "That." We must not divide our conception of the universe; for in dividing it, we have only fragmentary knowledge and we thus limit ourselves.

He who sees all beings in his Self and his Self in all beings, he never suffers; because when he sees all creatures within his true Self, then jealousy, grief and hatred vanish. He alone can love. That AH-pervading One is self- effulgent, birthless, deathless, pure, untainted by sin and sorrow. Knowing this, he becomes free from the bondage of matter and transcends death. Transcending death means realizing the difference between body and Soul and identifying oneself with the Soul. When we actually behold the undecaying Soul within us and realize our true nature, we no longer identify ourself with the body which dies and we do not die with the body.

Self-knowledge has always been the theme of the Sages; and the Upanishads deal especially with the knowledge of the Self and also with the knowledge of God, because there is no difference between the Self and God. They are one and the same. That which comes out of the Infinite Whole must also be infinite; hence the Self is infinite. That is the ocean, we are the drops. So long as the drop remains separate from the ocean, it is small and weak; but when it is one with the ocean, then it has all the strength of the ocean. Similarly, so long as man believes himself to be separate from the Whole, he is helpless; but when he identifies himself with It, then he transcends all weakness and partakes of Its omnipotent qualities.

Katha-Upanishad

The Katha-Upanishad is probably the most widely known of all the Upanishads. It was early translated into Persian and through this rendering first made its way into Europe. Later Raja Ram Mohun Roy brought out an English version. It has since appeared in various languages; and English, German and French writers are all agreed in pronouncing it one of the most perfect expressions of the religion and philosophy of the Vedas. Sir Edwin Arnold popularized it by his metrical rendering under the name of "The Secret of Death," and Ralph Waldo Emerson gives its story in brief at the close of his essay on "Immortality."

There is no consensus of opinion regarding the place of this Upanishad in Vedic literature. Some authorities declare it to belong to the Yajur-Veda, others to the Sama-Veda, while a large number put it down as a part of the Atharva-Veda. The story is first suggested in the Rig-Veda; it is told more definitely in the Yajur-Veda; and in the Katha-Upanishad it appears fully elaborated and interwoven with the loftiest Vedic teaching. There is nothing however, to indicate the special place of this final version, nor has any meaning been found for the name Katha.

The text presents a dialogue between an aspiring disciple, Nachiketas, and the Ruler of Death regarding the great Hereafter.

Katha-Upanishad

Peace Chant

May He (the Supreme Being) protect us both, teacher and taught. May He be pleased with us. May we acquire strength. May our study bring us illumination. May there be no enmity among us.

OM! PEACE! PEACE! PEACE!

Part First

I

Vahasrava, being desirous of heavenly rewards (at the Viswajit sacrifice), made a gift of all that he possessed. He had a son by the name of Nachiketas.

II

When the offerings were being distributed, faith (Shraddha) entered (the heart of)Nachiketas, who, though young, yet resected:

III

These cows have drunk water, eaten grass and given milk for the last time, and their senses have lost all vigour. He who gives these undoubtedly goes to joyless realms.

In India the idea of sacrifice has always been to give freely for the joy of giving, without asking anything in return; and the whole purpose and merit of the sacrifice is lost, if the giver entertains the least thought of name, fame or individual benefit. The special Viswajit sacrifice which Vajasrava was making required of him to give away all that he possessed. When, however, the gifts were brought forward to be offered, his son Nachiketas, although probably a lad about twelve years of age, observed how worthless were the animals which his father was offering. His heart at once became filled with Shraddha. There is no one English word which can convey the meaning of this Sanskrit term. It is more than mere faith. It also implies self-reliance, an independent sense of right and wrong, and the courage of one's own conviction. As a boy of tender age, Nachiketas had no right to question his father's action; yet, impelled by the sudden awakening of his higher nature, he could not but reflect: "By merely giving these useless cows, my father cannot gain any merit. If he has vowed to give all his possessions, then he must also give me. Otherwise his sacrifice will not be complete and fruitful." Therefore, anxious for his father's welfare, he approached him gently and reverently.

IV

He said to his father: Dear father, to whom wilt thou give me?
He said it a second time, then a third time. The father replied:
I shall give thee unto Death.

Nachiketas, being a dutiful son and eager to atone for his father's inadequate sacrifice, tried to remind him thus indirectly that he had not fulfilled his promise to give away all his possessions, since he had not yet offered his own son, who would be a worthier gift than useless cattle. His father, conscious that he was not making a true sacrifice, tried to ignore the boy's questions; but irritated by his persistence, he at last impatiently made answer: "I give thee to Yama, the Lord of Death." The fact that anger could so quickly rise in his heart proved that he had not the proper attitude of a sacrificer, who must always be tranquil, uplifted and free from egoism.

V

Nachiketas thought: Among many (of my father's pupils) I stand first; among many (others) I stand in the middle (but never last). What will be accomplished for my father by my going this day to Yama?

It was not conceit which led Nachiketas to consider his own standing and importance. He was weighing his value as a son and pupil in order to be able to judge whether or not he had merit enough to prove a worthy gift. Although he realized that his father's harsh reply was only the expression of a momentary outburst of anger; yet he believed that greater harm might befall his father, if his word was not kept. Therefore he sought to strengthen his father's resolution by reminding him of the transitory condition of life. He said:

VI

Look back to those who lived before and look to those who live now. Like grain the mortal decays and like grain again springs up (is reborn).

All things perish, Truth alone remains. Why then fear to sacrifice me also; Thus Nachiketas convinced his father that he should remain true to his word and send him to Yama, the Ruler of Death. Then Nachiketas went to the abode of Death, but Yama was absent and the boy waited without food or drink for three days. On Yama's return one of his household said to him:

VII

Like fire a Brahmana guest enters into houses. That fire is quenched by an offering. (Therefore) O Vaivaswata, bring water.

VIII

The foolish man in whose house a Brahmana guest remains without food, all his hopes and expectations, all the merit gained by his association with the holy, by his good words and deeds, all his sons and cattle, are destroyed.

According to the ancient Vedic ideal a guest is the representative of God and should be received with due reverence and honor. Especially is this the case with a Brahmana or a Sannyasin whose life is wholly consecrated to God. Any one who fails to give proper care to a holy guest brings misfortune on himself and his household. When Yama returned, therefore, one of the members of his household anxiously informed him of Nachiketas' presence and begged him to bring water to wash his feet, this being always the first service to an arriving guest.

IX

Yama said: O Brahmana! Revered guest! My salutations to thee. As thou hast remained three nights in my house without food, therefore choose three boons, O Brahmana.

X

Nachiketas said: May Gautama, my father, be free from anxious thought (about me). May he lose all anger (towards me) and be pacified in heart. May he know and welcome me when I am sent back by thee. This, O Death, is the first of the three boons I choose.

XI

Yama replied: Through my will Auddalaki Aruni (thy father) will know thee, and be again towards thee as before. He will sleep in peace at night. He will be free from wrath when he sees thee released from the mouth of death.

XII

Nachiketas said: In the realm of heaven there is no fear, thou (Death) art not there; nor is there fear of old age. Having crossed beyond both hunger and thirst and being above grief, (they) rejoice in heaven.

XIII

Thou knowest, O Death, the fire-sacrifice that leads to heaven. Tell this to me, who am full of Shraddha (faith and yearning). They who live in the realm of heaven enjoy freedom from death. This I beg as my second boon.

XIV

Yama replied: I know well that fire which leads to the realm of heaven. I shall tell it to thee. Listen to me. Know, O Nachiketas, that this is the means of attaining endless worlds and their support. It is hidden in the heart of all beings.

XV

Yama then told him that fire-sacrifice, the beginning of all the worlds; what bricks, how many and how laid for the altar. Nachiketas repeated all as it was told to him. Then Death, being pleased with him, again said:

XVI

The great-soured Yama, being well pleased, said to him (Nachiketas): I give thee now another boon. This fire (sacrifice) shall be named after thee. Take also this garland of many colours.

XVII

He who performs this Nachiketa fire-sacrifice three times, being united with the three (mother, father and teacher), and who fulfills the three-fold duty (study of the Vedas, sacrifice and alms-giving) crosses over birth and death. Knowing this worshipful shining fire, born of Brahman, and realizing Him, he attains eternal peace.

XVIII

He who knows the three-fold Nachiketa fire and performs the Nachiketa fire-sacrifice with three-fold knowledge, having cast off the fetters of death and being beyond grief, he rejoices in the realm of heaven.

XIX

O Nachiketas, this is thy fire that leads to heaven, which thou hast chosen as thy second boon. People will call this fire after thy name. Ask the third boon, Nachiketas.

Fire is regarded as "the foundation of all the worlds," because it is the revealer of creation. If there were no fire or light, no manifested form would be visible. We read in the Semitic Scriptures, "In the beginning the Lord said, 'Let there be light.'" Therefore, that which stands in the external universe as one of the purest symbols of the Divine, also dwells in subtle form in the heart of every living being as the vital energy, the life-force or cause of existence.

Yama now tells Nachiketas how, by performing sacrifice with the three-fold knowledge, he may transcend grief and death and reach heaven. The three-fold knowledge referred to is regarding the preparation of the altar and fire. Nachiketas being eager to learn, listened with wholehearted attention and was able to repeat all that was told him. This so pleased Yama that he granted him the extra boon of naming the fire-sacrifice after him and gave him a garland set with precious stones.

Verses XVI-XVIII are regarded by many as an interpolation, which would account for certain obscurities and repetitions in them.

XX

Nachiketas said: There is this doubt regarding what becomes of a man after death. Some say he exists, others that he does not exist. This knowledge I desire, being instructed by thee. Of the boons this is the third boon.

XXI

Yama replied: Even the Devas (Bright Ones) of old doubted regarding this. It is not easy to know; subtle indeed is this subject. O Nachiketas, choose another boon. Do not press me. Ask not this boon of me.

XXII

Nachiketas said: O Death, thou sayest that even the Devas had doubts about this, and that it is not easy to know. Another teacher like unto thee is not to be found. Therefore no other boon can be equal to this one.

XXIII

Yama said: Ask for sons and grandsons who shall live a hundred years, many cattle, elephants, gold and horses. Ask for lands of vast extent and live thyself as many autumns as thou desirest.

XXIV

If thou thinkest of any other boon equal to this, ask for wealth and long life; be ruler over the wide earth. O Nachiketas, I shall make thee enjoyer of all desires.

XXV

Whatsoever objects of desire are difficult to obtain in the realm of mortals, ask them all as thou desirest; these lovely maidens with their chariots and musical instruments, such as are not obtainable by mortals--be served by these whom I give to thee. O Nachiketas, do not ask regarding death.

The third boon asked by Nachiketas concerning the great Hereafter was one which could be granted only to those who were freed from all mortal desires and limitations, therefore Yama first tested Nachiketas to see whether he was ready to receive such knowledge. "Do not press me regarding this secret," he said. "Even wise men cannot understand it and thou art a mere lad. Take, rather, long life, wealth, whatever will give thee happiness on the mortal plane." But the boy proved his strength and worthiness by remaining firm in his resolution to know the great secret of life and death.

XXVI

Nachiketas said: O Death, these are fleeting; they weaken the vigour of all the senses in man. Even the longest life is short. Keep thou thy chariots, dance and music.

XXVII

Man cannot be satisfied by wealth. Shall we possess wealth when we see thee (Death)? Shall we continue to live as long as thou rulest? Therefore that boon alone is to be chosen by me.

XXVIII

What man dwelling on the decaying mortal plane, having approached the undecaying immortal one, and having reflected upon the nature of enjoyment through beauty and sense pleasure, would delight in long life?

XXIX

O Death, that regarding which there is doubt, of the great Hereafter, tell us. Nachiketas asks for no other boon than that which penetrates this hidden secret.

Part Second

I

Yama said: The good is one thing and the pleasant another. These two, having different ends, bind a man. It is well with him who chooses the good. He who chooses the pleasant misses the true end.

II

The good and the pleasant approach man; the wise examines both and discriminates between them; the wise prefers the good to the pleasant, but the foolish man chooses the pleasant through love of bodily pleasure.

III

O Nachiketas after wise reflection thou hast renounced the pleasant and all pleasing forms. Thou hast not accepted this garland of great value for which many mortals perish.

IV

Wide apart are these two,--ignorance and what is known as wisdom, leading in opposite directions. I believe Nachiketas to be one who longs for wisdom, since many tempting objects have not turned thee aside.

With this second part, the Ruler of Death begins his instructions regarding the great Hereafter. There are two paths,--one leading Godward, the other leading to worldly pleasure. He who follows one inevitably goes away from the other; because, like light and darkness they conflict. One leads to the imperishable spiritual realm; the other to the perishable physical realm. Both confront a man at every step of life. The discerning man distinguishing between the two, chooses the Real and Eternal, and he alone attains the highest, while the ignorant man, preferring that which brings him immediate and tangible results, misses the true purpose of his existence. Although Yama put before Nachiketas many temptations to test his sincerity and earnestness, he judging them at their real value, refused them all, saying "I have come from the mortal realm, shall I ask for what is mortal? I desire only that which is eternal." Then Death said to him: "I now see that thou art a sincere desirer of Truth. I offered thee vast wealth, long life and every form of pleasure which tempts and deludes men; but thou hast proved thy worthiness by rejecting them all."

V

Fools dwelling in ignorance, yet imagining themselves wise and learned, go round and round in crooked ways, like the blind led by the blind.

VI

The Hereafter never rises before the thoughtless child (the ignorant), deluded by the glamour of wealth. "This world alone is, there is none other": thinking thus, he falls under my sway again and again.

There are many in the world, who, puffed up with intellectual conceit, believe that they are capable of guiding others. But although they may possess a certain amount of worldly wisdom, they are devoid of deeper understanding; therefore all that they say merely increases doubt and confusion in the minds of those who hear them. Hence they are likened to blind men leading the blind.

The Hereafter does not shine before those who are lacking in the power of discrimination and are easily carried away therefore by the charm of fleeting objects. As children are tempted by toys, so they are tempted by pleasure, power, name and fame. To them these seem the only realities. Being thus attached to perishable things, they come many times under the dominion of death. There is one part of us which must die; there is another part which never dies. When a man can identify himself with his undying nature, which is one with God, then he overcomes death.

VII

He about whom many are not even able to hear, whom many cannot comprehend even after hearing: wonderful is the teacher, wonderful is he who can receive when taught by an able teacher.

Throughout the Vedic Scriptures it is declared that no one can impart spiritual knowledge unless he has realization. What is meant by realization?

It means knowledge based on direct perception. In India often the best teachers have no learning, but their character is so shining that every one learns merely by coming in contact with them. In one of the Scriptures we read: Under a banyan tree sat a youthful teacher and beside him an aged disciple. The mind of the disciple was full of doubts and questions, but although the teacher continued silent, gradually every doubt vanished from the disciple's mind. This signifies that the conveying of spiritual teaching does not depend upon words only. It is the life, the illumination, which counts. Such God-enlightened men, however, cannot easily be found; but even with such a teacher, the knowledge of the Self cannot be gained unless the heart of the disciple is open and ready for the Truth. Hence Yama says both teacher and taught must be wonderful.

VIII

When taught by a man of inferior understanding, this Atman cannot be truly known, even though frequently thought upon. There is no way (to know It) unless it is taught by another (an illumined teacher), for it is subtler than the subtle and beyond argument.

IX

O Dearest, this Atman cannot be attained by argument; It is truly known only when taught by another (a wise teacher). O Nachiketas, thou hast attained It. Thou art fixed in Truth. May we ever, find a questioner like thee.

Knowledge of the Atman or Self cannot be attained when it is taught by those who themselves lack in real understanding of It; and who therefore, having no definite conviction of their own, differ among themselves as to its nature and existence. Only he who has been able to perceive the Self directly, through the unfoldment of his higher nature, can proclaim what It actually is; and his words alone carry weight and bring illumination. It is too subtle to be reached by argument. This secret regarding the Hereafter cannot be known through reasoning or mere intellectual gymnastics. It is to be attained only in a state of consciousness which transcends the boundary line of reason.

X

I know that (earthly) treasure is transitory, for the eternal can never be attained by things which are non-eternal. Hence the Nachiketa fire (sacrifice) has been performed by me with perishable things and yet I have attained the eternal.

XI

O Nachiketas, thou hast seen the fulfillment of all desires, the basis of the universe, the endless fruit of sacrificial rites, the other shore where there is no fear, that which is praiseworthy, the great and wide support; yet, being wise, thou hast rejected all with firm resolve.

The teacher, saying that the imperishable cannot be attained by the perishable, shows that no amount of observance of rituals and ceremonies can earn the imperishable and eternal. Although the Nachiketa fire-sacrifice may bring results which seem eternal to mortals because of their long duration, yet they too must come to an end; therefore this sacrifice cannot lead to the final goal. Yama praises Nachiketas because, when all heavenly and earthly pleasures, as well as knowledge of all realms and their enjoyments were offered him, yet he cast them aside and remained firm in his desire for Truth alone.

XII

The wise, who by means of the highest meditation on the Self knows the Ancient One, difficult to perceive, seated in the innermost recess, hidden in the cave of the heart, dwelling in the depth of inner being, (he who knows that One) as God, is liberated from the fetters of joy and sorrow.

XIII

A mortal, having heard and fully grasped this, and having realized through discrimination the subtle Self, rejoices, because he has obtained that which is the source of all joy. I think the abode (of Truth) is open to Nachiketas.

The Scriptures give three stages in all spiritual attainment. The aspirant must first hear about the Truth from an enlightened teacher; next he must reflect upon what he has heard; then by constant practice of discrimination and meditation he realizes it; and with realization comes the fulfillment of every desire, because it unites him with the source of all. Having beheld this, a man learns that all sense pleasures are but fragmentary reflections of that one supreme joy, which can be found in the true Self alone. Yama assures Nachiketas that there is no doubt of his realizing the Truth, because he has shown the highest discrimination as well as fixity of purpose.

XIV

Nachiketas said: That which thou seest, which is neither virtue nor vice, neither cause nor effect, neither past nor future (but beyond these), tell me That.

XV

Yama replied: That goal which all the Vedas glorify, which all austerities proclaim, desiring which (people) practice Brahmacharya (a life of continence and service), that goal I tell thee briefly--it is Aum.

What name can man give to God? How can the Infinite be bound by any finite word? All that language can express must be finite, since it is itself finite. Yet it is very difficult for mortals to think or speak of anything without calling it by a definite name. Knowing this, the Sages gave to the Supreme the name A-U-M which stands as the root of all language. The first letter "A" is the mother-sound, being the natural sound uttered by every creature when the throat is opened, and no sound can be made without opening the throat. The last letter "M," spoken by closing the lips, terminates all articulation. As one carries the sound from the throat to the lips, it passes through the sound "U." These three sounds therefore cover the whole field of possible articulate sound. Their combination is called the Akshara or the imperishable word, the Sound-Brahman or the Word God, because it is the most universal name which can be given to the Supreme. Hence it must be the word which was "in the beginning" and corresponds to the Logos of Christian theology. It is because of the all-embracing significance of this name that it is used so universally in the Vedic Scriptures to designate the Absolute.

XVI

This Word is indeed Brahman. This Word is indeed the Supreme. He who knows this Word obtains whatever he desires.

XVII

This is the best Support, This is the highest Support; he who knows this Support is glorified in the world of Brahman.

This sacred Word is the highest symbol of the Absolute. He who through meditating on It grasps Its full significance, realizes the glory of God and at once has all his desires satisfied, because God is the fulfillment of all desires.

XVIII

This Self is never born, nor does It die. It did not spring from anything, nor did anything spring from It. This Ancient One is unborn, eternal, everlasting. It is not slain even though the body is slain.

XIX

If the slayer thinks that he slays, or if the slain thinks that he is slain, both of these know not. For It neither slays nor is It slain.

XX

The Self is subtler than the subtle, greater than the great; It dwells in the heart of each living being. He who is free from desire and free from grief, with mind and senses tranquil, beholds the glory of the Atman.

Although this Atman dwells in the heart of every living being, yet It is not perceived by ordinary mortals because of Its subtlety. It cannot be perceived by the senses; a finer spiritual sight is required. The heart must be pure and freed from every unworthy selfish desire; the thought must be indrawn from all external objects; mind and body must be under control; when the whole being thus becomes calm and serene, then it is possible to perceive that effulgent Atman. It is subtler than the subtle, because It is the invisible essence of every thing; and It is greater than the great because It is the boundless, sustaining power of the whole universe; that upon which all existence rests.

XXI

Though sitting, It travels far; though lying, It goes everywhere. Who else save me is fit to know that God, who is (both) joyful and joyless?

The Self is all-pervading, hence It is that which sits still and that which travels, that which is active and that which is inactive. It is both stationary and moving, and It is the basis of all forms of existence; therefore whatever exists in the universe, whether joy or joylessness, pleasure or pain, must spring from It. Who is better able to know God than I myself, since He resides in my heart and is the very essence of my being?

Such should be the attitude of one who is seeking.

XXII

The wise who know the Self, bodiless, seated within perishable bodies, great and all- pervading, grieve not.

Then a wise man through the practice of discrimination has seen clearly the distinction between body and Soul, he knows that his true Self is not the body, though It dwells in the body. Thus realizing the indestructible, all-pervading nature of his real Self, he surmounts all fear of death or loss, and is not moved even by the greatest sorrow.

XXIII

This Self cannot be attained by study of the Scriptures, nor by intellectual perception, nor by frequent hearing (of It); He whom the Self chooses, by him alone is It attained. To him the Self reveals Its true nature.

We may imagine that by much study we can find out God; but merely hearing about a thing and gaining an intellectual comprehension of it does not mean attaining true knowledge of it. Knowledge only comes through direct perception, and direct perception of God is possible for those alone who are pure in heart and spiritually awakened. Although He is alike to all beings and His mercy is on all, yet the impure and worldy-minded do not get the blessing, because they do not know how to open their hearts to it. He who longs for God, him the Lord chooses; because to him alone can He reveal His true nature.

XXIV

He who has not turned away from evil conduct, whose senses are uncontrolled, who is not tranquil, whose mind is not at rest, he can never attain this Atman even by knowledge.

Yama having first described what the Atman is, now tells us how to attain It. Man must try to subdue his lower nature and gain control over the body and senses. He must conquer the impure selfish desires which now disturb the serenity of his mind, that it may grow calm and peaceful. In other words, he must live the life and develop all spiritual qualities in order to perceive the Atman.

XXV

Who then can know where is this mighty Self? He (that Self) to whom the Brahmanas and Kshatriyas are but food and death itself a condiment.

This text proclaims the glory and majesty of the Supreme. The

Brahmanas stand for spiritual strength, the Kshatriyas for physical strength, yet both are overpowered by His mightiness. Life and death alike are food for Him. As the light of the great sun swallows up all the lesser lights of the universe, similarly all worlds are lost in the effulgence of the Eternal Omnipresent Being.

Part Third

I

There are two who enjoy the fruits of their good deeds in the world, having entered into the cave of the heart, seated (there) on the highest summit. The knowers of Brahman call them shadow and light. So also (they are called) by householders who perform five fire- sacrifices or three Nachiketa fire-sacrifices.

Here the two signify the Higher Self and the lower self, dwelling in the innermost cave of the heart. The Seers of Truth, as well as householders who follow the path of rituals and outer forms with the hope of enjoying the fruits of their good deeds, both proclaim that the Higher Self is like a light and the lower self like a shadow. When the Truth shines clearly in the heart of the knower, then he surmounts the apparent duality of his nature and becomes convinced that there is but One, and that all outer manifestations are nothing but reflections or projections of that One.

II

May we be able to learn that Nachiketa fire-sacrifice, which is a bridge for those who perform sacrifice. May we also know the One, who is the highest imperishable Brahman for those who desire to cross over to the other shore which is beyond fear.

The significance of this text is May we acquire the knowledge of Brahman, the Supreme, in both manifested and unmanifested form. He is manifested as the Lord of sacrifice for those who follow the path of ritual He is the unmanifested, eternal, universal Supreme Being for those who follow the path of wisdom. The "other shore," being the realm of immortality, is said to be beyond fear; because disease, death, and all that which mortals fear, cease to exist there. It is believed by many that these two opening verses were a later interpolation.

III

Know the Atman (Self) as the lord of the chariot, and the body as the chariot. Know also the intellect to be the driver and mind the reins.

IV

The senses are called the horses; the sense objects are the roads; when the Atman is united with body, senses and mind, then the wise call Him the enjoyer.

In the third chapter Yama defines what part of our being dies and what part is deathless, what is mortal and what is immortal. But the Atman, the Higher Self, is so entirely beyond human conception that it is impossible to give a direct definition of It. Only through similies can some idea of It be conveyed. That is the reason why all the great Teachers of the world have so often taught in the form of parables. So here the Ruler of Death represents the Self as the lord of this chariot of the body. The intellect or discriminative faculty is the driver, who controls these wild horses of the senses by holding firmly the reins of the mind. The roads over which these horses travel are made up of all the external objects which attract or repel the senses:--the sense of smelling follows the path of sweet odours, the sense of seeing the way of beautiful sights. Thus each sense, unless restrained by the discriminative faculty, seeks to go out towards its special objects. When the Self is joined with body, mind and senses, It is called the intelligent enjoyer; because It is the one who wills, feels, perceives and does everything.

V

He who is without discrimination and whose mind is always uncontrolled, his senses are unmanageable, like the vicious horses of a driver.

VI

But he who is full of discrimination and whose mind is always controlled, his senses are manageable, like the good horses of a driver.

The man whose intellect is not discriminative and who fails to distinguish right from wrong, the real from the unreal, is carried away by his sense passions and desires, just as a driver is carried away by vicious horses over which he has lost control. But he who clearly distinguishes what is good from what is merely pleasant, and controls all his out-going forces from running after apparent momentary pleasures, his senses obey and serve him as good horses obey their driver.

VII

He who does not possess discrimination, whose mind is

uncontrolled and always impure, he does not reach that goal, but falls again into Samsara (realm of birth and death).

VIII

But he who possesses right discrimination, whose mind is under control and always pure, he reaches that goal, from which he is not born again.

IX

The man who has a discriminative intellect for the driver, and a controlled mind for the reins, reaches the end of the journey, the highest place of Vishnu (the All-pervading and Unchangeable One).

A driver must possess first a thorough knowledge of the road; next he must understand how to handle the reins and control his horses. Then will he drive safely to his destination. Similarly in this journey of life, our mind and senses must be wholly under the control of our higher discriminative faculty; for only when all our forces work in unison can we hope to reach the goal—the abode of Absolute Truth.

X

Beyond the senses are the objects, beyond the objects is the mind, beyond the mind is the intellect, beyond the intellect is the great Atman.

XI

Beyond the great Atman is the Unmanifested; beyond the Unmanifested is the Purusha (the Cosmic Soul); beyond the Purusha there is nothing. That is the end, that is the final goal.

In these two verses the Teacher shows the process of discrimination, by which one attains knowledge of the subtle Self. Beginning with the sense-organs, he leads up to the less and less gross, until he reaches that which is subtlest of all, the true Self of man. The senses are dependent on sense-objects, because without these the senses would have no utility. Superior to sense-objects is the mind, because unless these objects affect the mind, they cannot influence the senses. Over the mind the determinative faculty exercises power; this determinative faculty is governed by the individual Self; beyond this Self is the undifferentiated creative energy known as Avyaktam; and above this is the Purusha or Supreme Self. Than this there is nothing higher. That is the goal, the Highest Abode of Peace and Bliss.

XII

This Atman (Self), hidden in all beings, does not shine forth;
but It is seen by subtle seers through keen and subtle
understanding.

If It dwells in all living beings, why do we not see It? Because the ordinary man's vision is too dull and distracted. It is visible to those alone whose intellect has been purified by constant thought on the Supreme, and whose sight therefore has become refined and sharpened. This keenness of vision comes only when all our forces have been made one-pointed through steadfast practice of concentration and meditation.

XIII

A wise man should control speech by mind, mind by intellect,
intellect by the great Atman, and that by the Peaceful One (the
Paramatman or Supreme Self).

Here Yama gives the practical method to be followed if one wishes to realize the Supreme. The word "speech" stands for all the senses. First, therefore, a man must control his outgoing senses by the mind. Then the mind must be brought under the control of the discriminative faculty; that is, it must be withdrawn from all sense-objects and cease to waste its energies on nonessential things. The discriminative faculty in turn must be controlled by the higher individual intelligence and this must be governed wholly by the Supreme Intelligence.

XIV

A rise! Awake! Having reached the Great Ones (illumined Teachers), gain understanding. The path is as sharp as a razor, impassable and difficult to travel, so the wise declare.

This is the eternal call of the wise: Awake from the slumber of ignorance! Arise and seek out those who know the Truth, because only those who have direct vision of Truth are capable of teaching It. Invoke their blessing with a humble spirit and seek to be instructed by them. The path is very difficult to tread. No thoughtless or lethargic person can safely travel on it. One must be strong, wakeful and persevering.

XV

Knowing That which is soundless, touchless, formless, undecaying; also tasteless, odorless, and eternal; beginningless, endless and immutable; beyond the Unmanifested: (knowing That) man escapes from the mouth of death.

The Ruler of Death defines here the innermost essence of our being. Because of its extreme subtlety, it cannot be heard or felt or smelled or tasted like any ordinary object. It never dies. It has no beginning or end. It is unchangeable. Realizing this Supreme Reality, man escapes from death and attains everlasting life. Thus the Teacher has gradually led Nachiketas to a point where he can reveal to him the secret of death. The boy had thought that there was a place where he could stay and become immortal. But Yama shows him that immortality is a state of consciousness and is not gained so long as man clings to name and form, or to perishable objects. What dies? Form. Therefore the formful man dies; but not that which dwells within. Although inconceivably subtle, the Sages have always made an effort through similies and analogies to give some idea of this inner Self or the God within. They have described It as beyond mind and speech; too subtle for ordinary perception, but not beyond the range of purified vision.

XVI

The intelligent man, who has heard and repeated the ancient story of Nachiketas, told by the Ruler of Death, is glorified in the world of Brahman.

XVII

He who with devotion recites this highest secret of immortality before an assembly of Brahmanas (pious men) or at the time of Shraddha (funeral ceremonies), gains everlasting reward, he gains everlasting reward.

Part Fourth

I

The Self-existent created the senses out-going; for this reason man sees the external, but not the inner Atman (Self). Some wise man, however, desiring immortality, with eyes turned away (from the external) sees the Atman within.

In the last chapter the Ruler of Death instructed Nachiketas regarding the nature and glory of the Self. Now he shows the reason why the Self is not seen by the majority. It is because man's mind is constantly drawn outward through the channels of his senses, and this prevents his seeing the inner Self (Pratyagatman); but now and then a seeker, wiser than others, goes within and attains the vision of the undying Self.

II

Children (the ignorant) pursue external pleasures; (thus) they fall into the wide- spread snare of death. But the wise, knowing the nature of immortality, do not seek the permanent among fleeting things.

Those who are devoid of discrimination and fail to distinguish between real and unreal, the fleeting and the permanent, set their hearts on the changeable things of this world; hence they entangle themselves in the net of insatiable desire, which leads inevitably to disappointment and suffering. To such, death must seem a reality because they identify themselves with that which is born and which dies. But the wise, who see deeper into the nature of things, are no longer deluded by the charm of the phenomenal world and do not seek for permanent happiness among its passing enjoyments.

III

That by which one knows form, taste, smell, sound, touch and sense enjoyments, by That also one knows whatever remains (to be known). This verily is That (which thou hast asked to know).

IV

That by which a mortal perceives, both in dream and in waking, by knowing that great all-pervading Atman the wise man grieves no more.

In these verses the teacher tries to make plain that all knowledge, as well as all sense perception, in every state of consciousness--sleeping, dreaming or waking--is possible only because the Self exists. There can be no knowledge or perception independent of the Self. Wise men, aware of this, identify themselves with their Higher Self and thus transcend the realm of grief.

V

He who knows this Atman, the honey-eater (perceiver and enjoyer of objects), ever near, as the lord of the past and future, fears no more. This verily is That.

VI

He who sees Him seated in the five elements, born of Tapas (fire of Brahman), born before water; who, having entered the cave of the heart, abides therein --this verily is That.

This verse indicates that He, the Great Self, is the cause of all created objects. According to the Vedas, His first manifestation was Brahma, the Personal God or Creator, born of the fire of wisdom. He existed before the evolution of the five elements--earth, water, fire, air and ether; hence He was "born before water." He is the Self dwelling in the hearts of all creatures.

VII

He who knows Aditi, who rises with Prana (the Life Principle), existent in all the Devas; who, having entered into the heart, abides there; and who was born from the elements--this verily is That.

This verse is somewhat obscure and seems like an interpolated amplification of the preceding verse.

VIII

Tje all-seeing fire which exists hidden in the two sticks, as the foetus is well-guarded in the womb by the mother, (that fire) is to be worshipped day after day by wakeful seekers (after wisdom), as well as by sacrificers. This verily is That.

Fire is called all-seeing because its light makes everything visible. In Vedic sacrifices the altar fire was always kindled by rubbing together two sticks of a special kind of wood called Arani. Because fire was regarded as one of the most perfect symbols of Divine wisdom, it was to be worshipped by all seekers after Truth, whether they followed the path of meditation or the path of rituals.

IX

From whence the sun rises, and whither it goes at setting, upon That all the Devas depend. No one goes beyond That. This verily is That.

X

What is here (in the visible world), that is there (in the invisible); he who sees difference (between visible and invisible) goes from death to death.

XI

By mind alone this is to be realized. There is no difference whatever (between visible and invisible). He who sees difference here (between these) goes from death to death.

In the sight of true wisdom, there is no difference between the creator and the created. Even physical science has come to recognize that cause and effect are but two aspects of one manifestation of energy. He who fails to see this, being engrossed in the visible only, goes from death to death; because he clings to external forms which are perishable. Only the essence which dwells within is unchangeable and imperishable. This knowledge of the oneness of visible and invisible, however, cannot be acquired through sense-perception. It can only be attained by the purified mind.

XII

The Purusha (Self), of the size of a thumb, resides in the middle of the body as the lord of the past and the future, (he who knows Him) fears no more. This verily is That.

The seat of the Purusha is said to be the heart, hence It "resides in the middle of the body." Although It is limitless and all-pervading, yet in relation to Its abiding-place It is represented as limited in extension, "the size of a thumb." This refers really to the heart, which in shape may be likened to a thumb. s light is everywhere, yet we see it focused in a lamp and believe it to be there only; similarly, although the life-current flows everywhere in the body, the heart is regarded as peculiarly its seat.

XIII

That Purusha, of the size of a thumb, is like a light without smoke, lord of the past and the future. He is the same today and tomorrow. This verily is That.

In this verse the teacher defines the effulgent nature of the Soul, whose light is pure like a flame without smoke. He also answers the question put by Nachiketas as to what happens after death, by declaring that no real change takes place, because the Soul is ever the same.

XIV

As rain water, (falling) on the mountain top, runs down over the rocks on all sides; similarly, he who sees difference (between visible forms) runs after them in various directions.

XV

O Gautama (Nachiketas), as pure water poured into pure water becomes one, so also is it with the Self of an illumined Knower (he becomes one with the Supreme).

Part Fifth

I

The city of the Unborn, whose knowledge is unchanging, has eleven gates. Thinking on Him, man grieves no more; and being freed (from ignorance), he attains liberation. This verily is That.

This human body is called a city with eleven gates, where the eternal unborn Spirit dwells. These gates are the two eyes, two ears, two nostrils, the mouth, the navel, the two lower apertures, and the imperceptible opening at the top of the head. The Self or Atman holds the position of ruler in this city; and being above the modifications of birth, death and all human imperfections, It is not affected by the changes of the physical organism. As the intelligent man through constant thought and meditation realizes the splendour of this Supreme Spirit, he becomes free from that part of his nature which grieves and suffers, and thus he attains liberation.

II

He is the sun dwelling in the bright heaven; He is the air dwelling in space; He is the fire burning on the altar; He is the guest dwelling in the house. He dwells in man. He dwells in those greater than man. He dwells in sacrifice. He dwells in the ether. He is (all that is) born in water, (all that) is born in earth, (all that) is born in sacrifice, (all that) is born on mountains. He is the True and the Great.

III

He it is who sends the (in-coming) Prana (life-breath) upward and throws the (out-going) breath downward. Him all the senses worship, the adorable Atman, seated in the centre (the heart).

IV

When this Atman, which is seated in the body, goes out (from the body), what remains then? This verily is That.

V

No mortal lives by the in-coming breath (Prana) or by the out-going breath (Apana), but he lives by another on which these two depend.

VI

O Gautama (Nachiketas), I shall declare unto thee the secret of the eternal Brahman and what happens to the Self after death.

VII

Some Jivas (individual Souls) enter wombs to be embodied; others go into immovable forms, according to their deeds and knowledge.

This text shows the application of the law of cause and effect to all forms of life. The thoughts and actions of the present life determine the future birth and environment.

VIII

The Being who remains awake while all sleep, who grants all desires, That is pure, That is Brahman, That alone is said to be immortal. On That all the worlds rest. None goes beyond That. This verily is That.

IX

As fire, though one, having entered the world, becomes various according to what it burns, so does the Atman (Self) within all living beings, though one, become various according to what it enters. It also exists outside.

X

As air, though one, having entered the world, becomes various according to what it enters, so does the Atman within all living beings, though one, become various according to what it enters. It also exists outside.

By using these similies of fire and air, the teacher tries to show Nachiketas the subtle quality of the great Self, who, although one and formless like air and fire, yet assumes different shapes according to the form in which It dwells. But, being all-pervading and unlimited, It cannot be confined to these forms; therefore it is said that It also exists outside all forms.

XI

As the sun, the eye of the whole world, is not defiled by

external impurities seen by the eyes, thus the one inner Self of all living beings is not defiled by the misery of the world, being outside it.

The sun is called the eye of the world because it reveals all objects. As the sun may shine on the most impure object, yet remain uncontaminated by it, so the Divine Self within is not touched by the impurity or suffering of the physical form in which it dwells, the Self being beyond all bodily limitations.

XII

There is one ruler, the Self of all living beings, who makes the one form manifold; the wise who perceive Him seated within their Self, to them belongs eternal bliss, not to others.

XIII

Eternal among the changing, consciousness of the conscious, who, though one, fulfils the desires of many: the wise who perceive Him seated within their Self, to them belongs eternal peace, not to others.

XIV

They (the wise) perceive that indescribable highest bliss, saying, This is That. How am I to know It? Does It shine (by Its own light) or does It shine (by reflected light)?

XV

The sun does not shine there, nor the moon, nor the stars; nor do these lightnings shine there, much less this fire. When He shines, everything shines after Him; by His light all is lighted.

Part Sixth

I

This ancient Aswattha tree has its root above and branches below. That is pure, That is Brahman, That alone is called the Immortal. All the worlds rest in That. None goes beyond That. This verily is That.

This verse indicates the origin of the tree of creation (the Samsara-Vriksha), which is rooted above in Brahman, the Supreme, and sends its branches downward into the phenomenal world. Heat and cold, pleasure and pain, birth and death, and all the shifting conditions of the mortal realm--these are the branches; but the origin of the tree, the Brahman, is eternally pure, unchanging, free and deathless. From the highest angelic form to the minutest atom, all created things have their origin in Him. He is the foundation of the universe. There is nothing beyond Him.

II

Whatever there is in the universe is evolved from Prana and vibrates in Prana. That is a mighty terror, like an upraised thunderbolt. They who know That become immortal.

III

From fear of Him the fire burns, from fear of Him the sun shines. From fear of Him Indra and Vayu and Death, the fifth, speed forth.

Just as the body cannot live or act without the Soul, similarly nothing in the created world can exist independent of Brahman, who is the basis of all existence. His position is like that of a king whom all must obey; hence it is said that the gods of sun, moon, wind, rain, do His bidding. He is likened to an upraised thunderbolt, because of the impartial and inevitable nature of

His law, which all powers, great or small, must obey absolutely.

IV

Ifa man is not able to know Him before the dissolution of the body, then he becomes embodied again in the created worlds.

As soon as a man acquires knowledge of the Supreme, he is liberated; but if he fails to attain such knowledge before his Soul is separated from the body, then he must take other bodies and return again and again to this realm of birth and death, until through varied experience he realizes the nature of the Supreme and his relation to Him.

V

As in a mirror, so is He seen within oneself; as in a dream, so (is He seen) in the world of the fathers (departed spirits); as in water, so (is He seen) in the world of Gandharvas (the angelic realm). As light and shadow, so (is He seen) in the world of Brahma (the Creator).

When by means of a purified understanding one beholds God

within, the image is distinct as in a polished mirror; but one cannot have clear vision of the Supreme by attaining to the various realms known as heavens, where one reaps the fruit of his good deeds. It is only by developing one's highest consciousness here in this life that perfect God-vision can be attained.

VI

Knowing that the senses are distinct (from the Atman) and their rising and setting separate (from the Atman), a wise man grieves no more.

A wise man never confounds the Atman, which is birthless and deathless, with that which has beginning and end. Therefore, when he sees his senses and his physical organism waxing and waning, he knows that his real Self within can never be affected by these outer changes, so he remains unmoved.

VII

Higher than the senses is the mind, higher than the mind is the intellect, higher than the intellect is the great Atman, higher than the Atman is the Unmanifested.

VIII

Beyond the Unmanifested is the all-pervading and imperceptible Being (Purusha). By knowing Him, the mortal is liberated and attains immortality.

This division of the individual into senses, mind, intellect, self-consciousness, undifferentiated creative energy and the Absolute Self is explained in the commentary of verse XI, Part Third.

IX

His form is not to be seen. No one can see Him with the eye. He is perceived by the heart, by the intellect and by the mind. They who know this become immortal.

The Supreme, being formless, cannot be discerned by the senses, hence all knowledge of Him must be acquired by the subtler faculties of heart, intellect and mind, which are developed only through the purifying practice of meditation.

X

When the five organs of perception become still, together with the mind, and the intellect ceases to be active: that is called the highest state.

The teacher now shows Nachiketas the process by which the transcendental vision can be attained. he out-going senses,--seeing, hearing, smelling, touching, tasting; the restless mind and the intellect: all must be indrawn and quieted. The state of equilibrium thus attained is called the highest state, because all the forces of one's being become united and focused; and this inevitably leads to supersensuous vision.

XI

This firm holding back of the senses is what is known as Yoga. Then one should become watchful, for Yoga comes and goes.

Yoga literally means to join or to unite the lower self with the Higher Self, the object with the subject, the worshipper with God. In order to gain this union, however, one must first disunite oneself from all that scatters the physical, mental and intellectual forces; so the outgoing perceptions must be detached from the external world and indrawn. When this is accomplished through constant practice of concentration and meditation, the union takes place of its own accord. But it may be lost again, unless one is watchful.

XII

He cannot be attained by speech, by mind, or by the eye. How can That be realized except by him who says "He is"?

XIII

He should be realized as "He is" and also as the reality of both (visible and invisible). He who knows Him as "He is," to him alone His real nature is revealed.

This supersensuous vision cannot be gained through man's ordinary faculties. By mind, eye, or speech the manifested attributes of the Divine can be apprehended; but only one who has acquired the supersensuous sight can directly perceive God's existence and declare definitely that "He is," that He alone exists in both the visible and the invisible world.

XIV

When all desires dwelling in the heart cease, then the mortal becomes immortal and attains Brahman here.

XV

When all the ties of the heart are cut asunder here, then the mortal becomes immortal. Such is the teaching.

XVI

There are a hundred and one nerves of the heart. One of them penetrates the centre of the head. Going upward through it, one attains immortality. The other (hundred nerve-courses) lead, in departing, to different worlds.

The nervous system of the body provides the channels through which the mind travels; the direction in which it moves is determined by its desires and tendencies. When the mind becomes pure and desireless, it takes the upward course and at the time of departing passes out through the imperceptible opening at the crown of the head; but as long as it remains full of desires, its course is downward towards the realms where those desires can be satisfied.

XVII

The Purusha, the inner Self, of the size of a thumb, is ever seated in the heart of all living beings. With perseverance man should draw Him out from his body as one draws the inner stalk from a blade of grass. One should know Him as pure and deathless, as pure and deathless.

As has been explained in Part Fourth, verse XII, the inner Self, although unlimited, is described as "the size of a thumb" because of its abiding-place in the heart, often likened to a lotus-bud which is similar to a thumb in size and shape. Through the process of steadfast discrimination, one should learn to differentiate the Soul from the body, just as one separates the pith from a reed.

XVIII

Thus Nachiketas, having acquired this wisdom taught by the Ruler of Death, together with all the rules of Yoga, became free from impurity and death and attained Brahman (the Supreme). So also will it be with another who likewise knows the nature of the

Self.

PEACE CHANT

May He (the Supreme Being) protect us both. May He be pleased with us. May we acquire strength. May our study bring us illumination. May there be no enmity among us.

OM! PEACE! PEACE! PEACE!

Here ends this Upanishad

Kena-Upanishad

Like the Isavasya, this Upanishad derives its name from the opening word of the text, Kena-ishitam, "by whom directed." It is also known as the Talavakara-Upanishad because of its place as a chapter in the Talavakara-Brahmana of the Sama-Veda.

Among the Upanishads it is one of the most analytical and metaphysical, its purpose being to lead the mind from the gross to the subtle, from effect to cause. By a series of profound questions and answers, it seeks to locate the source of man's being; and to expand his self-consciousness until it has become identical with God-Consciousness.

KENA-UPANISHAD

Peace Chant

May my limbs, speech, Prana (life-force), sight, hearing, strength and all my senses, gain in vigor. All is the Brahman (Supreme Lord) of the Upanishads. May I never deny the Brahman. May the Brahman never deny me. May there be no denial of the Brahman. May there be no separation from the Brahman. May all the virtues declared in the sacred Upanishads be manifest in me, who am devoted to the Atman (Higher Self). May they be manifest in me.

OM! PEACE! PEACE! PEACE!

Part First

I

By whom commanded and directed does the mind go towards its objects? Commanded by whom does the life-force, the first (cause), move? At whose will do men utter speech? What power directs the eye and the ear?

Thus the disciple approached the Master and inquired concerning the cause of life and human activity. Having a sincere longing for Truth he desired to know who really sees and hears, who actuates the apparent physical man. He perceived all about him the phenomenal world, the existence of which he could prove by his senses; but he sought to know the invisible causal world, of which he was now only vaguely conscious. Is mind all-pervading and all-powerful, or is it impelled by some other force, he asked. Who sends forth the vital energy, without which nothing can exist? The teacher replies:

II

It is the ear of the ear, the mind of the mind, the speech of the speech, the life of the life, the eye of the eye. The wise, freed (from the senses and from mortal desires), after leaving this world, become immortal.

An ordinary man hears, sees, thinks, but he is satisfied to know only as much as can be known through the senses; he does not analyze and try to find that which stands behind the ear or eye or mind. He is completely identified with his external nature. His conception does not go beyond the little circle of his bodily life, which concerns the outer man only. He has no consciousness of that which enables his senses and organs to perform their tasks.

There is a vast difference between the manifested form and That which is manifested through the form. When we know That, we shall not die with the body. One who clings to the senses and to things that are ephemeral, must die many deaths, but that man who knows the eye of the eye, the ear of the ear, having severed himself from his physical nature, becomes immortal. Immortality is attained when man transcends his apparent nature and finds that subtle, eternal and inexhaustible essence which is within him.

III

There the eye does not go, nor speech, nor mind. We do not know That; we do not understand how It can be taught. It is distinct from the known and also It is beyond the unknown. Thus we have heard from the ancient (teachers) who told us about It.

These physical eyes are unable to perceive that subtle essence. Nor can it be expressed by finite language or known by finite intelligence, because it is infinite. Our conception of knowing finite things is to know their name and form; but knowledge of God must be distinct from such knowledge. This is why some declare God to be unknown and unknowable; because He is far more than eyeor mind or speech can perceive, comprehend or express. The Upanishad does not say that He cannot be known. He is unknowable to man's finite nature. How can a finite mortal apprehend the Infinite Whole? But He can be known by man's God-like nature.

IV

That which speech does not illumine, but which illumines speech: know that alone to be the Brahman (the Supreme Being), not this which people worship here.

V

That which cannot be thought by mind, but by which, they say, mind is able to think: know that alone to be the Brahman, not this which people worship here.

VI

That which is not seen by the eye, but by which the eye is able to see: know that alone to be the Brahman, not this which people worship here.

VII

That which cannot be heard by the ear, but by which the ear is able to hear: know that alone to be Brahman, not this which people worship here.

VIII

That which none breathes with the breath, but by which breath is in-breathed: know that alone to be the Brahman, not this which people worship here.

Ordinarily we know three states of consciousness only,--waking, dreaming and sleeping. There is, however, a fourth state, the superconscious, which transcends these. In the first three states the mind is not clear enough to save us from error; but in the fourth state it gains such purity of vision that it can perceive the Divine. If God could be known by the limited mind and senses, then God-knowledge would be like any other knowledge and spiritual science like any physical science. He can be known, however, by the purified mind only. Therefore to know God, man must purify himself. The mind described in the Upanishads is the superconscious mind. According to the Vedic Sages the mind in its ordinary state is only another sense organ. This mind is limited, but when it becomes illumined by the light of the Cosmic Intelligence, or the "mind of the mind," then it is able to apprehend the First Cause or That which stands behind all external activities.

Part Second

I

If thou thinkest "I know It well," then it is certain that thou knowest but little of the Brahman (Absolute Truth), or in what form He (resideth) in the Devas (minor aspects of Deity). Therefore I think that what thou thinkest to be known is still to be sought after.

Having given the definition of the real Self or Brahman, by which mortals are able to see, hear, feel and think, the teacher was afraid that the disciple, after merely hearing about It, might conclude that he knew It. So he said to him: "You have heard about It, but that is not enough. You must experience It. Mere intellectual recognition will not give you true knowledge of It. Neither can It be taught to you. The teacher can only show the way. You must find It for yourself."

Knowledge means union between subject and object. To gain this union one must practice, theory cannot help us. The previous chapter has shown that the knowledge of Brahman is beyond sense-perception: "There the eye does not go, nor speech, nor mind." "That is distinct from known and also It is beyond the unknown." Therefore it was necessary for the teacher to remind the disciple that knowledge based on sense-perception or intellectual apprehension should not be confounded with supersensuous knowledge. Although the disciple had listened to the teacher with unquestioning mind and was intellectually convinced of the truth of his words, it was now necessary for him to prove by his own experience what he had heard. Guided by the teacher, he sought within himself through meditation the meaning of Brahman; and having gained a new vision, he approached the teacher once more.

II

The disciple said: I do not think I know It well, nor do I think that I do not know It. He among us who knows It truly, knows (what is meant by) "I know" and also what is meant by "I know It not."

This appears to be contradictory, but it is not. In the previous chapter we learned that Brahman is "distinct from the known" and "beyond the unknown."

The disciple, realizing this, says: "So far as mortal conception is concerned, I do not think I know, because I understand that It is beyond mind and speech; yet from the higher point of view, I cannot say that I do not know; for the very fact that I exist, that I can seek It, shows that I know; for It is the source of my being. I do not know, however, in the sense of knowing the whole Infinite Ocean of existence." The word knowledge is used ordinarily to signify acquaintance with phenomena only, but man must transcend this relative knowledge before he can have a clear conception of God. One who wishes to attain Soul-consciousness must rise above matter.

The observation of material science being confined to the sense plane, it ignores what is beyond. Therefore it must always be limited and subject to change. It discovered atoms, then it went further and discovered electrons, and when it had found the one, it had to drop the other; so this kind of knowledge can never lead to the ultimate knowledge of the Infinite, because it is exclusive and not inclusive. Spiritual science is not merely a question of mind and brain, it depends on the awakening of our latent higher consciousness.

III

He who thinks he knows It not, knows It. He who thinks he knows It, knows It not. The true knowers think they can never know It (because of Its infinitude), while the ignorant think they know It.

By this text the teacher confirms the idea that Brahman is unthinkable, because unconditioned. Therefore he says: He who considers It beyond thought, beyond sense-perception, beyond mind and speech, he alone has a true understanding of Brahman. They who judge a living being from his external form and sense faculties, know him not; because the real Self of man is not manifested in his seeing, hearing, speaking. His real Self is that within by which he hears and speaks and sees. In the same way he knows not Brahman who thinks he knows It by name and form. The arrogant and foolish man thinks he knows everything; but the true knower is humble. He says: "How can I know Thee, who art Infinite and beyond mind and speech?" In the last portion of the text, the teacher draws an impressive contrast between the attitude of the wise man who knows, but thinks he does not know; and that of the ignorant who does not know, but thinks he knows.

IV

It (Brahman) is known, when It is known in every state of consciousness. (Through such knowledge) one attains immortality. By attaining this Self, man gains strength; and by Self-knowledge immortality is attained.

We have learned from the previous text that the Brahman is unknown to those whose knowledge is limited to sense experience; but He is not unknown to those whose purified intelligence perceives Him as the basis of all states of consciousness and the essence of all things. By this higher knowledge a man attains immortality, because he knows that although his body may decay and die, the subtle essence of his being remains untouched. Such an one also acquires unlimited strength, because he identifies himself with the ultimate Source. The strength which comes from one's own muscle and brain or from one's individual power must be limited and mortal and therefore cannot lift one beyond death; but through the strength which Atma-gnana or Self-knowledge gives, immortality is reached. Whenever knowledge is based on direct perception of this undying essence, one transcends all fear of death and becomes immortal.

V

If one knows It here, that is Truth; if one knows It not here, then great is his loss. The wise seeing the same Self in all beings, being liberated from this world, become immortal.

Part Third

I

The Brahman once won a victory for the Devas. Through that victory of the Brahman, the Devas became elated. They thought, "This victory is ours. This glory is ours."

Brahman here does not mean a personal Deity. There is a Brahma, the first person of the Hindu Trinity; but Brahman is the Absolute, the One without a second, the essence of all. There are different names and forms which represent certain personal aspects of Divinity, such as Brahma the Creator, Vishnu the Preserver and Siva the Transformer; but no one of these can fully represent the Whole. Brahman is the vast ocean of being, on which rise numberless ripples and waves of manifestation. From the smallest atomic form to a Deva or an angel, all spring from that limitless ocean of Brahman, the inexhaustible Source of life. No manifested form of life can be independent of its source, just as no wave, however mighty, can be independent of the ocean. Nothing moves without that Power. He is the only Doer. But the Devas thought: "This victory is ours, this glory is ours."

II

The Brahman perceived this and appeared before them. They did not know what mysterious form it was.

III

They said to Fire: "O Jataveda (All-knowing)! Find out what mysterious spirit this is." He said: "Yes."

IV

He ran towards it and He (Brahman) said to him: "Who art thou?" "I am Agni, I am Jataveda," he (the Fire-god) replied.

V

Brahman asked: "What power resides in thee?" Agni replied: "I can burn up all whatsoever exists on earth."

VI

Brahman placed a straw before him and said: "Burn this." He (Agni) rushed towards it with all speed, but was not able to burn it. So he returned from there and said (to the Devas): "I was not able to find out what this great mystery is."

VII

Then they said to Vayu (the Air-god): "Vayu! Find out what this mystery is." He said: "Yes."

VIII

He ran towards it and He (Brahman) said to him: "Who art thou?" "I am Vayu, I am Matarisva (traveller of Heaven)," he (Vayu) said.

IX

Then the Brahman said: "What power is in thee?" Vayu replied: "I can blow away all whatsoever exists on earth."

X

Brahman placed a straw before him and said: "Blow this away." He (Vayu) rushed towards it with all speed, but was not able to blow it away. So he returned from there and said (to the Devas): "I was not able to find out what this great mystery is."

XI

Then they said to Indra: "O Maghavan (Worshipful One)! Find out what this mystery is." He said: "Yes"; and ran towards it, but it disappeared before him.

XII

Then he saw in that very space a woman beautifully adorned, Uma of golden hue, daughter of Haimavat (Himalaya). He asked: "What is this great mystery?"

Here we see how the Absolute assumes concrete form to give knowledge of Himself to the earnest seeker. Brahman, the impenetrable mystery, disappeared and in His place appeared a personal form to represent Him. This is a subtle way of showing the difference between the Absolute and the personal aspects of Deity. The Absolute is declared to be unknowable and unthinkable, but He assumes deified personal aspects to make Himself known to His devotees. Thus Uma, daughter of the Himalaya, represents that personal aspect as the offspring of the Infinite Being; while the Himalaya stands as the symbol of the Eternal, Unchangeable One.

Part fourth

I

She (Uma) said: "It is Brahman. It is through the victory of Brahman that ye are victorious." Then from her words, he (Indra) knew that it (that mysterious form) was Brahman.

Uma replied to Indra, "It is to Brahman that you owe your victory. It is through His power that you live and act. He is the agent and you are all only instruments in His hands. Therefore your idea that 'This victory is ours, this glory is ours,' is based on ignorance." At once Indra saw their mistake. The Devas, being puffed up with vanity, had thought they themselves had achieved the victory, whereas it was Brahman; for not even a blade of grass can move without His command.

II

Therefore these Devas,--Agni, Vayu and Indra--excel other Devas, because they came nearer to Brahman. It was they who first knew this spirit as Brahman.

III

Therefore Indra excels all other Devas, because he came nearest to Brahman, and because he first (before all others) knew this spirit as Brahman.

Agni, Vayu and Indra were superior to the other Devas because they gained a closer vision; and they were able to do this because they were purer; while Indra stands as the head of the Devas, because he realized the Truth directly, he reached Brahman. The significance of this is that whoever comes in direct touch with Brahman or the Supreme is glorified.

IV

Thus the teaching of Brahman is here illustrated in regard to the Devas. He dashed like lightning, and appeared and disappeared just as the eye winks.

The teaching as regards the Devas was that Brahman is the only Doer. He had appeared before them in a mysterious form; but the whole of the unfathomable Brahman could not be seen in any definite form; so at the moment of vanishing, He manifested more of His immeasurable glory and fleetness of action by a sudden dazzling flash of light.

V

Next (the teaching) is regarding Adhyatman (the embodied Soul). The mind seems to approach Him (Brahman). By this mind (the seeker) again and again remembers and thinks about Brahman.

Only by the mind can the seeker after knowledge approach Brahman, whose nature in glory and speed has been described as like unto a flash of lightning. Mind alone can picture the indescribable Brahman; and mind alone, being swift in its nature, can follow Him. It is through the help of this mind that we can think and meditate on Brahman; and when by constant thought of Him the mind becomes purified, then like a polished mirror it can reflect His Divine Glory.

VI

That Brahman is called Tadvanam (object of adoration). He is to be worshipped by the name Tadvanam. He who knows Brahman thus, is loved by all beings.

Brahman is the object of adoration and the goal of all beings. For this reason he should be worshipped and meditated upon as Tadvanam. Whoever knows Him in this aspect becomes one with Him, and serves as a clear channel through which the blessings of Brahman flow out to others. The knower of God partakes of all His lovable qualities and is therefore loved by all true devotees.

VII

The disciple asked: O Master, teach me the Upanishad. (The teacher replied:) The Upanishad has been taught thee. We have certainly taught thee the Upanishad about Brahman.

VIII

The Upanishad is based on tapas (practice of the control of body, mind and senses), dama (subjugation of the senses), karma (right performance of prescribed actions). The Vedas are its limbs. Truth is its support.

IX

He who knows this (wisdom of the Upanishad), having been

cleansed

of all sin, becomes established in the blissful, eternal and highest abode of Brahman, in the highest abode of Brahman.

Here ends this Upanishad.

This Upanishad is called Kena, because it begins with the inquiry: "By whom" (Kena) willed or directed does the mind go towards its object? From whom comes life? What enables man to speak, to hear and see? And the teacher in reply gives him the definition of Brahman, the Source and Basis of existence. The spirit of the Upanishads is always to show that no matter where we look or what we see or feel in the visible world, it all proceeds from one Source.

The prevailing note of all Vedic teaching is this: One tremendous Whole becoming the world, and again the world merging in that Whole. It also strives in various ways to define that Source, knowing which all else is known and without which no knowledge can be well established. So here the teacher replies: That which is the eye of the eye, the ear of the ear, that is the inexhaustible river of being which flows on eternally; while bubbles of creation rise on the surface, live for a time, then burst.

The teacher, however, warns the disciple that this eye, ear, mind, can never perceive It; for It is that which illumines speech and mind, which enables eye and ear and all sense-faculties to perform their tasks. "It is distinct from the known and also It is beyond the unknown." He who thinks he knows It, knows It not; because It is never known by those who believe that It can be grasped by the intellect or by the senses; but It can be known by him who knows It as the basis of all consciousness.

The knower of Truth says, "I know It not," because he realizes the unbounded, infinite nature of the Supreme. "Thou art this (the visible), Thou art That (the invisible), and Thou art all that is beyond," he declares. The ordinary idea of knowledge is that which is based on sense preceptions; but the knowledge of an illumined Sage is not confined to his senses. He has all the knowledge that comes from the senses and all that comes from Spirit.

The special purpose of this Upanishad is to give us the knowledge of the Real, that we may not come under the dominion of the ego by identifying ourselves with our body, mind and senses. Mortals become mortals because they fall under the sway of ego and depend on their own limited physical and mental strength. The lesson of the parable of the Devas and Brahman is that there is no real power, no real doer except God. He is the eye of the eye, the ear of the ear; and eyes, ears, and all our faculties have no power independent of Him. When we thus realize Him as the underlying Reality of our being, we transcend death and become immortal.

OM! PEACE! PEACE! PEACE!

End of The Upanishads, translated by Swami Paramananda

The Gospel of Thomas

Introduction

In the winter of 1945, in Upper Egypt, an Arab peasant was gathering fertilizer and topsoil for his crops. While digging in the soft dirt he came across a large earthen vessel. Inside were scrolls containing hitherto unseen books.

The scrolls were discovered near the site of the ancient town of Chenoboskion, at the base of a mountain named Gebel et-Tarif, near Hamra-Dum, in the vicinity of Naj 'Hammadi, about sixty miles from Luxor in Egypt. The texts were written in the Coptic language and preserved on papyrus sheets. The lettering style dated them as having been penned around the third or fourth century A.D. The Gospel of Thomas is the longest of the volumes consisting of between 114 and 118 verses. Recent study indicates that the original works, of which the scrolls are copies, may predate the four canonical gospels of Matthew, Mark, Luke, and John. The origin of The Gospel of Thomas is now thought to be from the first or second century A.D.

The peasant boy who found this treasure stood to be rewarded greatly. This could have been the discovery of a lifetime for his family, but the boy had no idea what he had. He took the scrolls home, where his mother burned some as kindling. Others were sold to the black market antique dealers in Cairo. It would be years until they found their way into the hands of a scholar. Part of the thirteenth codex was smuggled from Egypt to America. In 1955 the existence of the codex had reached the ears of Gilles Quispel, a professor of religion and history in the Netherlands. The race was on to find and translate the scrolls.

The introduction of the collected sayings of Jesus refers to the writer as "Didymus (Jude) Thomas." This is the same Thomas who doubted Jesus and was then told to place his hand within the breach in the side of the Savior. In the Gospel of St. John, he is referred to as "Didymus," which means "twin" in Greek. In Aramaic, the name "Jude" (or Judas) also carries the sense of "twin". The use of this title led some in the apocryphal tradition to believe that he was the brother and confidant of Jesus. However, when applied to Jesus himself, the literal meaning of "twin" must be rejected by orthodox Christianity as well as anyone adhering to the doctrine of the virgin birth of the only begotten son of God. The title is likely meant to signify that Thomas was a close confidant of Jesus.

Ancient church historians mention that Thomas preached to the Parthians in Persia and it is said he was buried in Edessa. Fourth century chronicles attribute the evangelization of India (Asia-Minor or Central Asia) to Thomas.

The texts, which some believe predate the four gospels, has a very Zen-like or Eastern flavor. Since it is widely held that the four gospels of Matthew, Mark, Luke, and John have a common reference in the basic text of Mark, it stands to reason that all follow the same general insight and language. Since scholars believe that the Gospel of Thomas predates the four main gospels, it can be assumed it was written outside the influences common to the other gospels. Although the codex found in Egypt is dated to the fourth century, the actual construction of the text of Thomas is placed by most Biblical scholars at about 70 - 150 A.D.

If Thomas wrote his gospel first, without input from Mark, and from the standpoint of Eastern exposure as a result of his sojourn into India, it could explain the "Eastern" quality of the text.

Moreover, there is some speculation that the sayings found in Thomas could be more accurate to the original intent and wording of Jesus than the other gospels. This may seem counter-intuitive until we realize that Christianity itself is an Eastern religion, albeit Middle-Eastern. Although, as it spread west the faith went through many changes to westernize or Romanize it…Jesus was both mystical and Middle-Eastern.

The Gospel of Thomas was most likely composed in Syria, where tradition holds the church of Edessa was founded by Judas Thomas, "The Twin" (Didymos). The gospel may well be the earliest written tradition in the Syriac church

The Gospel of Thomas is sometimes called a Gnostic gospel. The term "Gnostic" derives from "gnosis," which in Greek means "knowledge." Gnostics believed that knowledge is formed or found from a personal encounter with God brought about by inward or intuitive insight. They believed they were privy to a secret knowledge about the divine. It is this knowledge that leads to their name. It is possible that the roots of the Gnostic system pre-dates Christianity and found a suitable home in the mystical side of the Christian faith.

There are numerous references to the Gnostics in second century literature. Their form of Christianity was considered heresy by the early church fathers. It is from the writings condemning the group that we glean most of our information. They are alluded to in the Bible in 1 Tm 1:4 and 1 Tm 6:20, and possibly the entirety of Jude, as the writers of the Bible defended their theology against that of the Gnostics.

The Gospel Of Thomas

These are the secret sayings which the living Jesus has spoken and Judas who is also Thomas (the twin) (Didymos Judas Thomas) wrote.

1. And he said: Whoever finds the interpretation of these sayings will not taste death.

John 8:51 Very truly I tell you, whoever keeps my word will never see death.

2. Jesus said: Let he who seeks not stop seeking until he finds, and when he finds he will be troubled, and when he has been troubled he will marvel (be astonished) and he will reign over all and in reigning, he will find rest.

3. Jesus said: If those who lead you said to you: Behold, the Kingdom is in the sky, then the birds of the sky would enter before you. If they said to you: It is in the sea, then the fish of the sea would enter ahead you. But the Kingdom of God

exists within you and it exists outside of you. Those who come to know (recognize) themselves will find it, and when you come to know yourselves you will become known and you will realize that you are the children of the Living Father. Yet if you do not come to know yourselves then you will dwell in poverty and it will be you who are that poverty.

Luke 17:20 And when he was demanded of by the Pharisees, when the kingdom of God should come, he answered them and said, The kingdom of God cometh not with observation: Neither shall they say, Lo here! Lo There! For, behold, the kingdom of God is within you.

4. Jesus said: The person of old age will not hesitate to ask a little child of seven days about the place of life, and he will live. For many who are first will become last, (and the last will be first). And they will become one and the same.

Mark 9:35 He sat down, called the twelve, and said to them: Whoever wants to be first must be last of all and servant of all. 36 Then he took a little child and put it among them, and taking it in his arms, he said to them: 37 Whoever welcomes one such child in my name welcomes me, and whoever welcomes me welcomes not me but the one who sent me.

5. Jesus said: Recognize what is in front of your face, and what has been hidden from you will be revealed to you. For there is nothing hidden which will not be revealed (become manifest), and nothing buried that will not be raised.

Mark 4:2 For there is nothing hid, except to be made manifest; nor is anything secret, except to come to light.

Luke 12:3 Nothing is covered up that will not be revealed, or hidden that will not be known.

Matthew 10:26 So have no fear of them; for nothing is covered up that will not be uncovered, and nothing secret that will not become known.

6. His Disciples asked Him, how do you want us to fast, and how will we pray? And how will we be charitable (give alms), and what laws of diet will we maintain?

Jesus said: Do not lie, and do not practice what you hate, for

everything is in the plain sight of Heaven. For there is nothing concealed that will not become manifest, and there is nothing covered that will not be exposed.

Luke 11:1 He was praying in a certain place, and after he had finished, one of his disciples said to him, Lord, teach us to pray, as John taught his disciples.

7. Jesus said: Blessed is the lion that the man will eat, for the lion will become the man. Cursed is the man that the lion shall eat, and still the lion will become man.

Mathew 26:20-30 He who dipped his hand with me in the dish, the same will betray me. The Son of Man goes, even as it is written of him, but woe to that man through whom the Son of Man is betrayed! It would be better for that man if he had not been born. Judas, who betrayed him, answered, It isn't me, is it, Rabbi? He said to him, You said it. As they were eating, Jesus took bread, gave thanks for it, and broke it. He gave to the disciples, and said, Take, eat; this is my body. He took the cup, gave thanks, and gave to them, saying: All of you drink it, for this is my blood of the new covenant, which is poured out for many for the remission of sins. But I tell you that I will not drink of this fruit of the vine from now on, until that day when I drink it anew with you in my Father's Kingdom. When they had sung a hymn, they went out to the Mount of Olives.

8. And he said: The Kingdom of Heaven is like a wise fisherman who casts his net into the sea. He drew it up from the sea full of small fish. Among them he found a fine large fish. That wise fisherman threw all the small fish back into the sea and chose the large fish without hesitation. Whoever has ears to hear, let him hear!

Matthew 13:47 Again, the kingdom of heaven is like a net that was thrown into the sea and caught fish of every kind; 48 when it was full, they drew it ashore, sat down, and put the good into baskets but threw out the bad.

9. Jesus said: Now, the sower came forth. He filled his hand and threw (the seeds). Some fell upon the road and the birds came and gathered them up. Others fell on the stone and they did not take deep enough roots in the soil, and so did not produce grain. Others fell among the thorns and they choked the seed, and the worm ate them. Others fell upon the good earth and it produced good fruit up toward the sky, it bore 60 fold and 120 fold.

Matthew 13:3 And he told them many things in parables, saying: Listen! A sower went out to sow. 4 And as he sowed, some seeds fell on the path, and the birds came and ate them up. 5 Other seeds fell on rocky ground, where they did not have much soil, and they sprang up quickly, since they had no depth of soil. 6 But when the sun rose, they were scorched; and since they had no root, they withered away. 7 Other seeds fell among thorns, and the thorns grew up and choked them. 8 Other seeds fell on good soil and brought forth grain, some a hundredfold, some sixty, some thirty.

Mark 4:2 And he taught them many things in parables, and in his teaching he said to them: 3 Behold! A sower went out to sow. 4 And as he sowed, some seed fell along the path, and the birds came and devoured it. 5 Other seed fell on rocky ground, where it had not much soil, and immediately it sprang up, since it had no depth of soil; 6 and when the sun rose it was scorched, and since it had no root it withered away. 7 Other seed fell among thorns and the thorns grew up and choked it, and it yielded no grain. 8 And other seeds fell into good soil and brought forth grain, growing up and increasing and yielding thirty fold and sixty fold and a hundredfold. 9 And he said, He who has ears to hear, let him hear.

Luke 8:4 And when a great crowd came together and people from town after town came to him, he said in a parable: 5 A sower went out to sow his seed; and as he sowed, some fell along the path, and was trodden under foot, and the birds of the air devoured it. 6 And some fell on the rock; and as it grew up, it withered away, because it had no moisture. 7 And some fell among thorns; and the thorns grew with it and choked it. 8 And some fell into good soil and grew, and yielded a hundredfold. As he said this, he called out, He who has ears to hear, let him hear.

10. Jesus said: I have cast fire upon the world and behold, I guard it until it is ablaze.

Luke 12:49 I came to bring fire to the earth, and how I wish it were already kindled.

11. Jesus said: This sky will pass away, and the one above it will pass away. The dead are not alive, and the living will not die. In the days when you consumed what is dead, you made it alive. When you come into the Light, what will you do? On the day when you were united (one), you became separated (two). When you have become separated (two), what will you do?

Matthew 24:35 Heaven and earth will pass away, but my words will not pass away.

12. The Disciples said to Jesus: We know that you will go away from us. Who is it that will be our teacher?

Jesus said to them: Wherever you are (in the place that you have come), you will go to James the Righteous, for whose sake Heaven and Earth were made (came into being).

13. Jesus said to his Disciples: Compare me to others, and tell me who I am like. Simon Peter said to him: You are like a righteous messenger (angel) of God. Matthew said to him: You are like a (wise) philosopher (of the heart). Thomas said to him: Teacher, my mouth is not capable of saying who you are like!

Jesus said: I'm not your teacher, now that you have drunk; you have become drunk from the bubbling spring that I have tended (measured out). And he took him, and withdrew and spoke three words to him: "ahyh ashr ahyh" (I am Who I am).

Now when Thomas returned to his comrades, they inquired of him: What did Jesus said to you? Thomas said to them: If I tell you even one of the words which he spoke to me, you will take up stones and throw them at me, and fire will come from the stones to consume you.

Mark 8:27 Jesus went on with his disciples to the villages of Caesarea Philippi; and on the way he asked his disciples, Who do people say that I am? 28 And they answered him, John the Baptist; and others, Elijah; and still others, one of the prophets. 29 He asked them, But who do you say that I am? Peter answered him, You are the Messiah. 30 And he sternly ordered them not to tell anyone about him.

14. Jesus said to them: If you fast, you will give rise to transgression (sin) for yourselves. And if you pray, you will be condemned. And if you give alms, you will cause harm (evil) to your spirits. And when you go into the countryside, if they take you in (receive you) then eat what they set before you and heal the sick among them. For what goes into your mouth will not defile you, but rather what comes out of your mouth, that is what will defile you.

Luke 10:8 Whenever you enter a town and its people welcome you, eat what is set before you; 9 Cure the sick who are there, and say to them, The kingdom of God has come near to you.

Mark 7:15 There is nothing outside a person that by going in can defile, but the things that come out are what defile.

Matthew 15:11 Not that what goes into the mouth defiles a man, but what comes out of the mouth, this defiles a man.

Romans 14.14 I know and am persuaded in the Lord Jesus that nothing is unclean in itself; but it is unclean for any one who thinks it unclean.

15. Jesus said: When you see him who was not born of woman, bow yourselves down upon your faces and worship him for he is your Father.

16. Jesus said: People think perhaps I have come to spread peace upon the world. They do not know that I have come to cast dissention (conflict) upon the earth; fire, sword, war. For

there will be five in a house. Three will be against two and two against three, the father against the son and the son against the father. And they will stand alone.

Matthew 10:34 Do not think that I have come to bring peace to the earth; I have not come to bring peace, but a sword. 35 For I have come to set a man against his father, and a daughter against her mother, and a daughter-in-law against her mother-in-law; 36 and one's foes will be members of one's own household.

Luke 12:51 Do you think that I have come to give peace on earth? No, I tell you, but rather division; 52 for henceforth in one house there will be five divided, three against two and two against three; 53 they will be divided, father against son and son against father, mother against daughter and daughter against her mother, mother-in-law against her daughter-in-law and daughter-in-law against her mother-in-law.

17. Jesus said: I will give to you what eye has not seen, what ear has not heard, what hand has not touched, and what has not occurred to the mind of man.

1 Cor 2:9 But, as it is written, What no eye has seen, nor ear heard, nor the human heart conceived, what God has prepared for those who love him.

18. The Disciples said to Jesus: Tell us how our end will come. Jesus said: Have you already discovered the beginning (origin), so that you inquire about the end? Where the beginning (origin) is, there the end will be. Blessed be he who will take his place in the beginning (stand at the origin) for he will know the end, and he will not experience death.

19. Jesus said: Blessed is he who came into being before he came into being. If you become my Disciples and heed my sayings, these stones will serve you. For there are five trees in paradise for you, which are undisturbed in summer and in winter and their leaves do not fall. Whoever knows them will not experience death.

20. The Disciples said to Jesus: Tell us what the Kingdom of Heaven is like. He said to them: It is like a mustard seed, smaller than all other seeds and yet when it falls on the tilled earth, it produces a great plant and becomes shelter for the birds of the sky.

Mark 4:30 He also said, With what can we compare the kingdom of God, or what parable will we use for it? 31 It is like a mustard seed, which, when sown upon the ground, is the smallest of all the seeds on earth; 32 yet when it is sown it grows up and becomes the greatest of all shrubs, and puts forth large branches, so that the birds of the air can make nests in its shade.

Matthew 13:31 The kingdom of heaven is like a grain of mustard seed which a man took and sowed in his field; 32 it is the smallest of all seeds, but when it has grown it is the greatest of shrubs and becomes a tree, so that the birds of the air come and make nests in its branches.

Luke 13.18 He said therefore, What is the kingdom of God like? And to what shall I compare it? 19 It is like a grain of mustard seed which a man took and sowed in his garden; and it grew and became a tree, and the birds of the air made nests in its branches.

21. Mary said to Jesus: Who are your Disciples like? He said: They are like little children who are living in a field that is not theirs. When the owners of the field come, they will say: Let us have our field! It is as if they were naked in front of

them (They undress in front of them in order to let them have what is theirs) and they give back the field. Therefore I said, if the owner of the house knows that the thief is coming, he will be alert before he arrives and will not allow him to dig through into the house to carry away his belongings. You, must be on guard and beware of the world (system). Prepare yourself (arm yourself) with great strength or the bandits will find a way to reach you, for the problems you expect will come. Let there be among you a person of understanding (awareness). When the crop ripened, he came quickly with his sickle in his hand to reap. Whoever has ears to hear, let him hear!

Matthew 24:43 But understand this: if the owner of the house had known in what part of the night the thief was coming, he would have stayed awake and would not have let his house be broken into.

Mark 4:26 He also said, The kingdom of God is as if someone would scatter seed on the ground, 27 and would sleep and rise night and day, and the seed would sprout and grow, he does not know how. 28 The earth produces of itself, first the stalk, then the head, then the full grain in the head. 29 But when the grain is ripe, at once he goes in with his sickle, because the harvest has come.

Luke 12:39 But know this, that if the householder had known at what hour the thief was coming, he would not have left his house to be broken into. 40 You also must be ready; for the Son of man is coming at an unexpected hour.

22. Jesus saw little children who were being suckled. He said to his Disciples: These little children who are being suckled are like those who enter the Kingdom.

They said to him: Should we become like little children in order to enter the Kingdom?

Jesus said to them: When you make the two one, and you make the inside as the outside and the outside as the inside, when you make the above as the below, and if you make the male and the female one and the same (united male and female) so that the man will not be masculine (male) and the female be not feminine (female), when you establish an eye in the place of an eye and a hand in the place of a hand and a

foot in the place of a foot and an likeness (image) in the place of a likeness (an image), then will you enter the Kingdom.

Luke 18:16 But Jesus called for them and said, Let the little children come to me, and do not stop them; for it is to such as these that the kingdom of God belongs. 17 Truly I tell you, whoever does not receive the kingdom of God as a little child will never enter it.

Mark 9:43 If your hand causes you to stumble, cut it off; it is better for you to enter life maimed than to have two hands and to go to hell, to the unquenchable fire. 45 And if your foot causes you to stumble, cut it off; it is better for you to enter life lame than to have two feet and to be thrown into hell. 47 And if your eye causes you to stumble, tear it out; it is better for you to enter the kingdom of God with one eye than to have two eyes and to be thrown into hell, 48 where their worm never dies, and the fire is never quenched.

Matthew 18:3 And said, Verily, I say unto you, unless you turn and become like children, you will never enter the kingdom of heaven. 4 Whoever humbles himself like this child, he is the greatest in the kingdom of heaven. 5 Whoever receives one such child in my name receives me;

Matthew 5:29 If your right eye causes you to sin, pluck it out and throw it away; it is better that you lose one of your members than that your whole body be thrown into hell. 30 And if your right hand causes you to sin, cut it off and throw it away; it is better that you lose one of your members than that your whole body go into hell.

23. Jesus said: I will choose you, one out of a thousand and two out of ten thousand and they will stand as a single one.

24. His Disciples said: Show us the place where you are (your place), for it is necessary for us to seek it.

He said to them: Whoever has ears, let him hear! Within a man of light there is light, and he illumines the entire world. If he does not shine, he is darkness (there is darkness).

John13:36 Simon Peter said to him, Lord, where are you going? Jesus answered, Where I am going, you cannot follow me now; but you will follow afterward.

Matthew 6:22 The eye is the lamp of the body. So, if your eye is healthy, your whole body will be full of light; 23 but if your eye is unhealthy, your whole body will be full of darkness. If then the light in you is darkness, how great is the darkness!

Luke 11:34 Your eye is the lamp of your body; when your eye is sound, your whole body is full of light; but when it is not sound, your body is full of darkness. 35 Therefore be careful lest the light in you be darkness. 36 If then your whole body is full of light, having no part dark, it will be wholly bright, as when a lamp with its rays gives you light.

25. Jesus said: Love your friend (Brother) as your soul; protect him as you would the pupil of your own eye.

26. Jesus said: You see the speck in your brother's eye but the beam that is in your own eye you do not see. When you remove the beam out of your own eye, then will you see clearly to remove the speck out of your brother's eye.

Matthew 7:3 Why do you see the speck in your neighbor's eye, but do not notice the log in your own eye? 4 Or how can you say to your neighbor, Let me take the speck out of your eye, while the log is in your own eye? 5 You hypocrite, first take the log out of your own eye, and then you will see clearly to take the speck out of your neighbor's eye.

Luke 6:41 Why do you see the speck that is in your brother's eye, but do not notice the log that is in your own eye? 42 Or how can you say to your brother, Brother, let me take out the speck that is in your eye, when you yourself do not see the log that is in your own eye? You hypocrite, first take the log out of your own eye, and then you will see clearly to take out the speck that is in your brother's eye.

27. Jesus said: Unless you fast from the world (system), you will not find the Kingdom of God. Unless you keep the Sabbath (entire week) as Sabbath, you will not see the Father.

28. Jesus said: I stood in the midst of the world. In the flesh I appeared to them. I found them all drunk; I found none thirsty among them. My soul grieved for the sons of men, for they are blind in their hearts and do not see that they came

into the world empty they are destined (determined) to leave the world empty. However, now they are drunk. When they have shaken off their wine, then they will repent (change their ways).

29. Jesus said: If the flesh came into being because of spirit, it is a marvel, but if spirit came into being because of the body, it would be a marvel of marvels. I marvel indeed at how great wealth has taken up residence in this poverty.

30. Jesus said: Where there are three gods, they are gods (Where there are three gods they are without god). Where there is only one, I say that I am with him. Lift the stone and there you will find me, Split the wood and there am I.

Matthew 18:20 For where two or three are gathered in my name, I am there among them.

31. Jesus said: No prophet is accepted in his own village, no physician heals those who know him.

Mark 6:4 Then Jesus said to them, Prophets are not without honor, except in their hometown, and among their own kin, and in their own house.

Matthew 13:57 And they took offense at him. But Jesus said to them: A prophet is not without honor save in his own country and in his own house.

Luke 4:24 And he said, Truly, I say to you, no prophet is acceptable in his own country.

John 4:43 After the two days he departed to Galilee. 44 For Jesus himself testified that a prophet has no honor in his own country.

32. Jesus said: A city being built (and established) upon a high mountain and fortified cannot fall nor can it be hidden.

Matthew 5:14 You are the light of the world. A city built on a hill cannot be hid.

33. Jesus said: What you will hear in your ear preach from your rooftops. For no one lights a lamp and sets it under a basket nor puts it in a hidden place, but rather it is placed up a lamp-stand so that everyone who comes and goes will see its light.

Matthew 10:27 What I say to you in the dark, tell in the light; and what you hear whispered, proclaim from the housetops.

Luke 8:16 No one after lighting a lamp hides it under a jar, or puts it under a bed, but puts it on a lamp stand, so that those who enter may see the light.

Matthew 5:15 Nor do men light a lamp and put it under a bushel, but on a stand, and it gives light to all in the house.

Mark 4:21 And he said to them, Is a lamp brought in to be put under a bushel, or under a bed, and not on a stand?

Luke 11:33 No one after lighting a lamp puts it in a cellar or under a bushel, but on a stand, that those who enter may see the light.

34. Jesus said: If a blind person leads a blind person, both fall into a pit.

Matthew 15:14 Let them alone; they are blind guides of the blind. And if one blind person guides another, both will fall into a pit.

Luke 6:39 He also told them a parable: Can a blind man lead a blind man? Will they not both fall into a pit?

35. Jesus said: It is impossible for anyone to enter the house of a strong man to take it by force unless he binds his hands, then he will be able to loot his house.

Matthew 12:29 Or how can one enter a strong man's house and plunder his goods, unless he first binds the strong man? Then indeed he may plunder his house.

Luke 11:21 When a strong man, fully armed, guards his own palace, his goods are in peace; 22 but when one stronger than he assails him and overcomes him, he takes away his armor in which he trusted, and divides his spoil.

Mark 3:27 But no one can enter a strong man's house and plunder his property without first tying up the strong man; then indeed the house can be plundered.

36. Jesus said: Do not worry from morning to evening nor from evening to morning about the food that you will eat nor about what clothes you will wear. You are much superior to the Lilies which neither card nor spin. When you have no clothing, what do you wear? Who can add time to your life (increase your stature)? He himself will give to you your garment.

Matthew 6:25 Therefore I tell you, do not worry about your life, what you will eat or what you will drink, or about your body, what you will wear. Is not life more than food, and the body more than clothing? 26 Look at the birds of the air; they neither sow nor reap nor gather into barns, and yet your heavenly Father feeds them. Are you not of more value than they? 27 And can any of you by worrying add a single hour to your span of life? 28 And why do you worry about clothing? Consider the lilies of the field, how they grow; they neither toil nor spin, 29 yet I tell you, even Solomon in all his glory was not clothed like one of these. 30 But if God so clothes the grass of the field, which is alive today and tomorrow is thrown into the oven, will he not much more clothe you--you of little faith? 31 Therefore do not worry, saying, What will we eat? or What will we drink? or What will we wear?

Luke 12:22 And he said to his disciples, Therefore I tell you, do not be anxious about your life, what you shall eat, nor about your body, what you shall put on. 23 For life is more than food, and the body more than clothing.

37. His Disciples said: When will you appear to us, and when will we see you?

Jesus said: When you take off your garments without being ashamed, and place your garments under your feet and tread on them as the little children do, then will you see the Son of the Living-One, and you will not be afraid.

38. Jesus said: Many times have you yearned to hear these sayings which I speak to you, and you have no one else from whom to hear them. There will be days when you will seek me but you will not find me.

39. Jesus said: The Pharisees and the Scribes have received the keys of knowledge, but they have hidden them. They did not go in, nor did they permit those who wished to enter to do so. However, you be as wise (astute) as serpents and innocent as doves.

Luke 11:52 Woe to you lawyers! For you have taken away the key of knowledge; you did not enter yourselves, and you hindered those who were entering.

Matthew 10:16 See, I am sending you out like sheep into the midst of wolves; so be wise as serpents and innocent as doves.

Matthew 23.13 But woe unto you, scribes and Pharisees, hypocrites! because you shut the kingdom of heaven against men; for you neither enter yourselves, nor allow those who would enter to go in.

40. Jesus said: A grapevine has been planted outside the (vineyard of the) Father, and since it is not viable (supported) it will be pulled up by its roots and destroyed.

Matthew 15:13 He answered, Every plant that my heavenly Father has not planted will be uprooted.

41. Jesus said: Whoever has (it) in his hand, to him will (more) be given. And whoever does not have, from him will be taken even the small amount which he has.

Matthew 25:29 For to all those who have, more will be given, and they will have an abundance; but from those who have nothing, even what they have will be taken away.

Luke 19:26 I tell you, that to every one who has will more be given; but from him who has not, even what he has will be taken away.

42. Jesus said: Become passers-by.

43. His Disciples said to him: Who are you, that you said these things to us?

Jesus said to them: You do not recognize who I am from what I said to you, but rather you have become like the Jews who either love the tree and hate its fruit, or love the fruit and hate the tree.

John 8:25 They said to him, Who are you? Jesus said to them, Why do I speak to you at all?

Matthew 7:16 You will know them by their fruits. Are grapes gathered from thorns, or figs from thistles? 17 In the same way, every good tree bears good fruit, but the bad tree bears bad fruit. 18 A good tree cannot bear bad fruit, nor can a bad tree bear good fruit. 19 Every tree that does not bear good fruit is cut down and thrown into the fire. 20 Thus you will know them by their fruits.

44. Jesus said: Whoever blasphemes against the Father, it will be forgiven him. And whoever blasphemes against the Son, it will be forgiven him. Yet whoever blasphemes against the Holy Spirit, it will not be forgiven him neither on earth nor in heaven.

Mark 3:28 Truly I tell you, people will be forgiven for their sins and whatever blasphemies they utter; 29 but whoever blasphemes against the Holy Spirit can never have forgiveness, but is guilty of an eternal sin.

Matthew 12:31 Therefore I tell you, every sin and blasphemy will be forgiven men, but the blasphemy against the Spirit will not be forgiven. 32 And whoever says a word against the Son of man will be forgiven; but whoever speaks against the Holy Spirit will not be forgiven, either in this age or in the age to come.

Luke 12:10 And every one who speaks a word against the Son of man will be forgiven; but he who blasphemes against the Holy Spirit will not be forgiven.

45. Jesus said: Grapes are not harvested from thorns, nor are figs gathered from thistles, for they do not give fruit. A good person brings forth goodness out of his storehouse. A bad person brings forth evil out of his evil storehouse which is in his heart, and he speaks evil, for out of the abundance of the

heart he brings forth evil.

Luke 6:43 For no good tree bears bad fruit, nor again does a bad tree bear good fruit; 44 for each tree is known by its own fruit. For figs are not gathered from thorns, nor are grapes picked from a bramble bush. 45 The good man out of the good treasure of his heart produces good, and the evil man out of his evil treasure produces evil; for out of the abundance of the heart his mouth speaks.

46. Jesus said: From Adam until John the Baptist there is none born of women who surpasses John the Baptist, so that his eyes should not be downcast (lowered). Yet I have said that whoever among you becomes like a child will know the Kingdom, and he will be greater than John.

Matthew 11:11 Truly I tell you, among those born of women no one has arisen greater than John the Baptist; yet the least in the kingdom of heaven is greater than he.

Luke 7:28 I tell you, among those born of women none is greater than John; yet he who is least in the kingdom of God is greater than he.

Matthew 18:2 He called a child, whom he put among them, 3 and said, Truly I tell you, unless you change and become like children, you will never enter the kingdom of heaven. 18:4 Whoever becomes humble like this child is the greatest in the kingdom of heaven.

47. Jesus said: It is impossible for a man to mount two horses or to draw two bows, and a servant cannot serve two masters, otherwise he will honor the one and disrespect the other. No man drinks vintage wine and immediately desires to drink new wine, and they do not put new wine into old wineskins or they would burst, and they do not put vintage wine into new wineskins or it would spoil (sour). They do not sew an old patch on a new garment because that would cause a split.

Matthew 6:24 No one can serve two masters; for a slave will either hate the one and love the other, or be devoted to the one and despise the other. You cannot serve God and wealth.

Matthew 9:16 No one sews a piece of unshrunk cloth on an old cloak, for the patch pulls away from the cloak, and a worse tear is made. 17

Neither is new wine put into old wineskins; otherwise, the skins burst, and the wine is spilled, and the skins are destroyed; but new wine is put into fresh wineskins, and so both are preserved.

Mark 2:21 No one sews a piece of unshrunk cloth on an old garment; if he does, the patch tears away from it, the new from the old, and a worse tear is made. 22 And no one puts new wine into old wineskins; if he does, the wine will burst the skins, and the wine is lost, and so are the skins; but new wine is for fresh skins.

Luke 5:36 He told them a parable also: No one tears a piece from a new garment and puts it upon an old garment; if he does, he will tear the new, and the piece from the new will not match the old. 37 And no one puts new wine into old wineskins; if he does, the new wine will burst the skins and it will be spilled, and the skins will be destroyed. 38 But new wine must be put into fresh wineskins. 39 And no one after drinking old wine desires new; for he says, The old is good.

48. Jesus said: If two make peace with each other in this one house, they will say to the mountain: Be moved! and it will be moved.

Matthew 18:19 Again, truly I tell you, if two of you agree on earth about anything you ask, it will be done for you by my Father in heaven.

Mark 11:23 Truly I tell you, if you say to this mountain, Be taken up and thrown into the sea, and if you do not doubt in your heart, but believe that what you say will come to pass, it will be done for you. 24 So I tell you, whatever you ask for in prayer, believe that you have received it, and it will be yours.

Matthew 17:20 He said to them, Because of your little faith. For truly, I say to you, if you have faith as a grain of mustard seed, you will say to this mountain, Move from here to there, and it will move; and nothing will be impossible to you.

49. Jesus said: Blessed is the solitary and chosen, for you will find the Kingdom. You have come from it, and unto it you will return.

50. Jesus said: If they said to you: From where do you come? Say to them: We have come from the Light, the place where the Light came into existence of its own accord and he stood and appeared in their image. If they said to you: Is it you? (Who are you?), say: We are his Sons and we are the chosen of the Living Father. If they ask you: What is the sign of your Father in you? Say to them: It is movement with rest.

51. His Disciples said to him: When will the rest of the dead occur, and when will the New World come? He said to them: That which you look for has already come, but you do not recognize it.

52. His Disciples said to him: Twenty-four prophets preached in Israel, and they all spoke of (in) you. He said to them: You have ignored the Living-One who is in your presence and you have spoken only of the dead.

53. His Disciples said to him: Is circumcision beneficial or not? He said to them: If it were beneficial, their father would beget them already circumcised from their mother. However, the true spiritual circumcision has become entirely beneficial.

54. Jesus said: Blessed be the poor, for yours is the Kingdom

of the Heaven.

Matthew 6:20 Then he looked up at his disciples and said: Blessed are you who are poor, for yours is the kingdom of God.

Luke 6:20 And he lifted up his eyes on his disciples, and said: Blessed are you poor, for yours is the kingdom of God.

Matthew 5:3 Blessed are the poor in spirit, for theirs is the kingdom of heaven.

55. Jesus said: Whoever does not hate his father and his mother will not be able to become my Disciple. And whoever does not hate his brothers and his sisters and does not take up his own cross in my way, will not become worthy of me.

Matthew 10:37 Whoever loves father or mother more than me is not worthy of me; and whoever loves son or daughter more than me is not worthy of me; 38 and whoever does not take up the cross and follow me is not worthy of me.

Luke 14:26 If any one comes to me and does not hate his own father and mother and wife and children and brothers and sisters, yes, and even his own life, he cannot be my disciple. 27 Whoever does not bear his own cross and come after me, cannot be my disciple.

56. Jesus said: Whoever has come to understand the world (system) has found a corpse, and whoever has found a corpse, is superior to the world (of him the system is not worthy).

57. Jesus said: The Kingdom of the Father is like a person who has good seed. His enemy came by night and sowed a weed among the good seed. The man did not permit them to pull up the weed, he said to them: perhaps you will intend to pull up the weed and you pull up the wheat along with it. But, on the day of harvest the weeds will be very visible and then they will pull them and burn them.

Matthew 13:24 He put before them another parable: The kingdom of heaven may be compared to someone who sowed good seed in his field; 25 but while everybody was asleep, an enemy came and sowed weeds among the wheat, and then went away. 26 So when the plants came up and bore grain, then the weeds appeared as well. 27 And the slaves of the householder came and said to him, Master, did you not sow good seed in your field? Where, then, did these weeds come from? 28 He answered, An enemy has done this. The slaves said to him, Then do you want us to go and gather them? 29 But he replied, No; for in gathering the weeds you would uproot the wheat along with them. 30 Let both of them grow together until the harvest; and at harvest time I will tell the reapers, Collect the weeds first and bind them in bundles to be burned, but gather the wheat into my barn.

58. Jesus said: Blessed is the person who has suffered, for he has found life. (Blessed is he who has suffered [to find life] and found life).

Matthew 11:28 Come to me, all you that are weary and are carrying heavy burdens, and I will give you rest.

59. Jesus said: Look to the Living-One while you are alive,

otherwise, you might die and seek to see him and will be unable to find him.

John 7:34 You will search for me, but you will not find me; and where I am, you cannot come.

John 13:33 Little children, I am with you only a little longer. You will look for me; and as I said to the Jews so now I say to you, Where I am going, you cannot come.

60. They saw a Samaritan carrying a lamb, on his way to Judea. Jesus said to them: Why does he take the lamb with him? They said to him: So that he may kill it and eat it. He said to them: While it is alive he will not eat it, but only after he kills it and it becomes a corpse. They said: How could he do otherwise? He said to them: Look for a place of rest for yourselves, otherwise, you might become corpses and be eaten.

61. Jesus said: Two will rest on a bed and one will die and the other will live. Salome said: Who are you, man? As if

sent by someone, you laid upon my bed and you ate from my table. Jesus said to her: "I-Am" he who is from that which is whole (the undivided). I have been given the things of my Father. Salome said: I'm your Disciple. Jesus said to her: Thus, I said that whenever someone is one (undivided) he will be filled with light, yet whenever he is divided (chooses) he will be filled with darkness.

Luke 17:34 I tell you, on that night there will be two in one bed; one will be taken and the other left.

62. Jesus said: I tell my mysteries to those who are worthy of my mysteries. Do not let your right hand know what your left hand is doing.

Mark 4:11 And he said to them, To you has been given the secret of the kingdom of God, but for those outside, everything comes in parables.

Matthew 6:3 But when you give alms, do not let your left hand know what your right hand is doing.

Luke 8:10 He said, To you it has been given to know the secrets of the kingdom of God; but for others they are in parables, so that seeing they may not see, and hearing they may not understand.

Matthew 13:10 Then the disciples came and said to him, Why do you speak to them in parables? 11 And he answered them, To you it has been given to know the secrets of the kingdom of heaven, but to them it has not been given.

63. Jesus said: There was a wealthy person who had much money, and he said: I will use my money so that I may sow and reap and replant, to fill my storehouses with grain so that I lack nothing. This was his intention (is what he thought in his heart) but that same night he died. Whoever has ears, let him hear!

Luke 12:16 Then he told them a parable: The land of a rich man produced abundantly. 17 And he thought to himself, What should I do, for I have no place to store my crops? 18 Then he said, I will do this: I will pull down my barns and build larger ones, and there I will store all my grain and my goods. 19 And I will say to my soul, Soul, you have ample goods laid up for many years; relax, eat, drink, be merry. 20 But God said to him, You fool! This very night your life is being demanded of you. And the things you have prepared, whose will they be? 21 So it is with those who store up treasures for themselves but are not rich toward God.

64. Jesus said: A person had houseguests, and when he had prepared the banquet in their honor he sent his servant to invite the guests. He went to the first, he said to him: My master invites you. He replied: I have to do business with some merchants. They are coming to see me this evening. I will go to place my orders with them. I ask to be excused from the banquet. He went to another, he said to him: My master has invited you. He replied to him: I have just bought a house and they require me for a day. I will have no spare time. He came to another, he said to him: My master invites you. He replied to him: My friend is getting married and I must arrange a banquet for him. I will not be able to come. I ask to be excused from the banquet. He went to another, he said to him: My master invites you. He replied to him: I have bought a farm. I go to receive the rent. I will not be able to come. I ask to be excused. The servant returned, he said to his

master: Those whom you have invited to the banquet have excused themselves. The master said to his servant: Go out to the roads, bring those whom you find so that they may feast. And he said: Businessmen and merchants will not enter the places of my Father.

Luke 14:16 Then Jesus said to him:, Someone gave a great dinner and invited many. 17 At the time for the dinner he sent his slave to say to those who had been invited, Come; for everything is ready now. 18 But they all alike began to make excuses. The first said to him, I have bought a piece of land, and I must go out and see it; please accept my regrets. 19 Another said, I have bought five yoke of oxen, and I am going to try them out; please accept my regrets. 20 Another said, I have just been married, and therefore I cannot come. 21 So the slave returned and reported this to his master. Then the owner of the house became angry and said to his slave, Go out at once into the streets and lanes of the town and bring in the poor, the crippled, the blind, and the lame. 22 And the slave said, Sir, what you ordered has been done, and there is still room. 23 Then the master said to the slave, Go out into the roads and lanes, and compel people to come in, so that my house may be filled. 24 For I tell you, none of those who were invited will taste my dinner.

Matthew 19:23 Then Jesus said to his disciples, Truly I tell you, it will be hard for a rich person to enter the kingdom of heaven.

Matthew 22:3 and sent his servants to call those who were invited to the marriage feast; but they would not come. 4 Again he sent other servants, saying, Tell those who are invited, Behold, I have made ready my dinner, my oxen and my fat calves are killed, and everything is ready; come to the marriage feast. 5 But they made light of it and went off, one to his farm, another to his business, 6 while the rest seized his servants, treated them shamefully, and killed them. 7 The king was angry, and he sent his troops and destroyed those murderers and burned their city. 8 Then he said to his servants, The wedding is ready, but those invited were not worthy. 9 Go therefore to the thoroughfares, and invite to the marriage feast as many as you find. 10 And those servants went out into the streets and gathered all whom they found, both bad and good; so the wedding hall was filled with guests. 11 But when the king came in to look at the guests, he saw there a man who had no wedding garment; 12 and he said to him, Friend, how did you get in here without a wedding garment? And he was speechless. 13 Then the king said to the attendants, Bind him hand and foot, and cast him into the outer darkness; there men will weep and gnash their teeth. 14 For many are called, but few are chosen.

65. He said: A kind person who owned a vineyard leased it to tenants so that they would work it and he would receive the fruit from them. He sent his servant so that the tenants would give to him the fruit of the vineyard. They seized his servant and beat him nearly to death. The servant went, he told his master what had happened. His master said: Perhaps they did not recognize him. So, he sent another servant. The tenants beat him also. Then the owner sent his son. He said: Perhaps they will respect my son. Since the tenants knew that he was the heir to the vineyard, they seized him and killed him. Whoever has ears, let him hear!

Matthew 21:33 Listen to another parable. There was a landowner who planted a vineyard, put a fence around it, dug a wine press in it, and built a watchtower. Then he leased it to tenants and went to another country. 34 When the harvest time had come, he sent his slaves to the tenants to collect his produce. 35 But the tenants seized his slaves and beat one, killed another, and stoned another. 36 Again he sent other slaves, more than the first; and they treated them in the same way. 37 Finally he sent his son to them, saying, They will respect my son. 38

But when the tenants saw the son, they said to themselves, This is the heir; come, let us kill him and get his inheritance. 39 So they seized him, threw him out of the vineyard, and killed him.

Mark 12:1 And he began to speak to them in parables. A man planted a vineyard, and set a hedge around it, and dug a pit for the wine press, and built a tower, and let it out to tenants, and went into another country. 2 When the time came, he sent a servant to the tenants, to get from them some of the fruit of the vineyard. 3 And they took him and beat him, and sent him away empty-handed. 4 Again he sent to them another servant, and they wounded him in the head, and treated him shamefully. 5 And he sent another, and him they killed; and so with many others, some they beat and some they killed. 6 He had still one other, a beloved son; finally he sent him to them, saying, They will respect my son. 7 But those tenants said to one another, This is the heir; come, let us kill him, and the inheritance will be ours. 8 And they took him and killed him, and cast him out of the vineyard. 9 What will the owner of the vineyard do? He will come and destroy the tenants, and give the vineyard to others.

Luke 20:9 And he began to tell the people this parable: A man planted a vineyard, and let it out to tenants, and went into another country for a long while. 10 When the time came, he sent a servant to the tenants, that they should give him some of the fruit of the vineyard; but the tenants beat him, and sent him away empty-handed. 11 And he sent another servant; him also they beat and treated shamefully, and sent him away empty-handed. 12 And he sent yet a third; this one they wounded and cast out. 13 Then the owner of the vineyard said, What shall I do? I will send my beloved son; it may be they will respect him. 14 But when the tenants saw him, they said to themselves, This is the heir; let us kill him, that the inheritance may be ours. 15 And they cast him out of the vineyard and killed him. What then will the owner of the vineyard do to them? 16 He will come and destroy those tenants, and give the vineyard to others. When they heard this, they said, God forbid!

66. Jesus said: Show me the stone which the builders have rejected. It is that one that is the cornerstone (keystone).

Matthew 21:42 Jesus said to them, Have you never read in the scriptures: The very stone which the builders rejected has become the head of the corner; this was the Lord's doing, and it is marvelous in our eyes?

Mark 12:10 Have you not read this scripture: The very stone which the builders rejected has become the head of the corner; 11 this was the

Lord's doing, and it is marvelous in our eyes?

Luke 20:17 But he looked at them and said, What then does this text mean: The stone that the builders rejected has become the cornerstone?

67. Jesus said: Those who know everything but themselves, lack everything. (whoever knows the all and still feels a personal lacking, he is completely deficient).

68. Jesus said: Blessed are you when you are hated and persecuted, but they themselves will find no reason why you have been persecuted.

Matthew 5:11 Blessed are you when people revile you and persecute you and utter all kinds of evil against you falsely on my account.

Luke 6:22 Blessed are you when men hate you, and when they exclude you and revile you, and cast out your name as evil, on account of the Son of man!

69. Jesus said: Blessed are those who have been persecuted in their heart these are they who have come to know the Father in truth. Jesus said: Blessed are the hungry, for the stomach of him who desires to be filled will be filled.

Matthew 5:8 Blessed are the pure in heart, for they will see God.

Luke 6:21 Blessed are you who are hungry now, for you will be filled.

70. Jesus said: If you bring forth what is within you, it will save you. If you do not have it within you to bring forth, that which you lack will destroy you.

71. Jesus said: I will destroy this house, and no one will be able to build it again.

Mark 14:58 We heard him say, I will destroy this temple that is made with hands, and in three days I will build another, not made with hands.

72. A person said to him: Tell my brothers to divide the possessions of my father with me. He said to him: Oh man, who made me a divider? He turned to his Disciples, he said

to them: I'm not a divider, am I?

Luke 12:13 Someone in the crowd said to him, Teacher, tell my brother to divide the family inheritance with me. 14 But he said to him, Friend, who set me to be a judge or arbitrator over you? 15 And he said to them, Take care! Be on your guard against all kinds of greed; for one's life does not consist in the abundance of possessions.

73. Jesus said: The harvest is indeed plentiful, but the workers are few. Ask the Lord to send workers for the harvest.

Matthew 9:37 Then he said to his disciples, The harvest is plentiful, but the laborers are few; 38 therefore ask the Lord of the harvest to send out laborers into his harvest.

74. He said: Lord, there are many around the well, yet there is nothing in the well. How is it that many are around the well and no one goes into it?

75. Jesus said: There are many standing at the door, but only those who are alone are the ones who will enter into the Bridal Chamber.

Matthew 22:14 For many are called, but few are chosen.

76. Jesus said: The Kingdom of the Father is like a rich merchant who found a pearl. The merchant was prudent. He sold his fortune and bought the one pearl for himself. You also, seek for his treasure which does not fail, which endures where no moth can come near to eat it nor worm to devour it.

Matthew 13:45 Again, the kingdom of heaven is like a merchant in search of fine pearls; 46 on finding one pearl of great value, he went and sold all that he had and bought it.

Matthew 6:19 Do not store up for yourselves treasures on earth, where moth and rust consume and where thieves break in and steal; 20 but store up for yourselves treasures in heaven, where neither moth nor rust consumes and where thieves do not break in and steal.

77. Jesus said: "I-Am" the Light who is over all things, "I-Am" the All. From me all came forth and to me all return (The All came from me and the All has come to me). Split

wood, there am I. Lift up the stone and there you will find me.

John 8:12 Again Jesus spoke to them, saying, I am the light of the world. Whoever follows me will never walk in darkness but will have the light of life.

John 1:3 All things came into being through him, and without him not one thing came into being.

78. Jesus said: Why did you come out to the wilderness; to see a reed shaken by the wind? And to see a person dressed in fine (soft - plush) garments like your rulers and your dignitaries? They are clothed in plush garments, and they are not able to recognize (understand) the truth.

Matthew 11:7 As they went away, Jesus began to speak to the crowds about John: What did you go out into the wilderness to look at? A reed shaken by the wind? 8 What then did you go out to see? Someone dressed in soft robes? Look, those who wear soft robes are in royal palaces. 9 What then did you go out to see? A prophet? Yes, I tell you, and more than a prophet.

79. A woman from the multitude said to him: Blessed is the womb which bore you, and the breasts which nursed you! He said to her: Blessed are those who have heard the word (meaning) of the Father and have truly kept it. For there will be days when you will say: Blessed be the womb which has not conceived and the breasts which have not nursed.

Luke 11:27 While he was saying this, a woman in the crowd raised her voice and said to him, Blessed is the womb that bore you and the breasts that nursed you! 28 But he said, Blessed rather are those who hear the word of God and obey it!

Luke 23:29 For the days are surely coming when they will say, Blessed are the barren, and the wombs that never bore, and the breasts that never nursed.

80. Jesus said: Whoever has come to understand (recognize) the world (world system) has found a corpse, and whoever has found the corpse, of him the world (world system) is not worthy.

81. Jesus said: Whoever has become rich should reign, and let whoever has power renounce it.

82. Jesus said: Whoever is close to me is close to the fire, and whoever is far from me is far from the Kingdom.

83. Jesus said: Images are visible to man but the light which is within them is hidden. The light of the father will be revealed, but he (his image) is hidden in the light.

84. Jesus said: When you see your reflection, you rejoice. Yet when you perceive your images which have come into being before you, which neither die nor can be seen, how much will you have to bear?

85. Jesus said: Adam came into existence from a great power and a great wealth, and yet he was not worthy of you. For if he had been worthy, he would not have tasted death.

86. Jesus said: The foxes have their dens and the birds have their nests, yet the Son of Man has no place to lay his head for rest.

Matthew 8:20 And Jesus said to him, Foxes have holes, and birds of the air have nests; but the Son of Man has nowhere to lay his head.

87. Jesus said: Wretched is the body which depends upon another body, and wretched is the soul which depends on these two (upon their being together).

88. Jesus said: The angels and the prophets will come to you, and what they will give you belongs to you. And you will give them what you have, and said among yourselves: When will they come to take (receive) what belongs to them?

89. Jesus said: Why do you wash the outside of your cup? Do you not understand (mind) that He who creates the inside is also He who creates the outside?

Luke 11:39 Then the Lord said to him, Now you Pharisees clean the outside of the cup and of the dish, but inside you are full of greed and wickedness. 40 You fools! Did not the one who made the outside make the inside also?

90. Jesus said: Come unto me, for my yoke is comfortable (natural) and my lordship is gentle— and you will find rest for yourselves.

Matthew 11:28 Come to me, all you that are weary and are carrying heavy burdens, and I will give you rest. 29 Take my yoke upon you, and learn from me; for I am gentle and humble in heart, and you will find rest for your souls. 30 For my yoke is easy, and my burden is light.

91. They said to him: Tell us who you are, so that we may believe in you. He said to them: You examine the face of the sky and of the earth, yet you do not recognize Him who is here with you, and you do not know how to seek in (to inquire of Him at) this moment (you do not know how to take advantage of this opportunity).

John 9:36 He answered, And who is he, sir? Tell me, so that I may believe in him.

Luke 12:54 He also said to the crowds, When you see a cloud rising in the west, you immediately say, It is going to rain; and so it happens. 55 And when you see the south wind blowing, you say, There will be scorching heat; and it happens. 56 You hypocrites! You know how to interpret the appearance of earth and sky, but why do you not know how to interpret the present time?

92. Jesus said: Seek and you will find. But in the past I did not answer the questions you asked. Now I wish to tell them to you, but you do not ask about (no longer seek) them.

Matthew 7:7 Ask, and it will be given you; search, and you will find; knock, and the door will be opened for you.

93. Jesus said: Do not give what is sacred to the dogs, lest they throw it on the dung heap. Do not cast the pearls to the swine, lest they cause it to become dung (mud).

Matthew 7:6 Do not give what is holy to dogs; and do not throw your pearls before swine, or they will trample them under foot and turn and maul you.

94. Jesus said: Whoever seeks will find. And whoever knocks, it will be opened to him.

Matthew 7:8 For everyone who asks receives, and everyone who searches finds, and for everyone who knocks, the door will be opened.

95. Jesus said: If you have money, do not lend at interest, but rather give it to those from whom you will not be repaid.

Luke 6:34 If you lend to those from whom you hope to receive, what credit is that to you? Even sinners lend to sinners, to receive as much again. 35 But love your enemies, do good, and lend, expecting nothing in return. Your reward will be great, and you will be children of the Most High; for he is kind to the ungrateful and the wicked.

96. Jesus said: The Kingdom of the Father is like a woman who has taken a little yeast and hidden it in dough. She produced large loaves of it. Whoever has ears, let him hear!

Matthew 13:33 He told them another parable: The kingdom of heaven is like yeast that a woman took and mixed in with three measures of flour until all of it was leavened.

97. Jesus said: The Kingdom of the Father is like a woman who was carrying a jar full of grain. While she was walking on a road far from home, the handle of the jar broke and the grain poured out behind her onto the road. She did not know it. She had noticed no problem. When she arrived in her house, she set the jar down and found it empty.

98. Jesus said: The Kingdom of the Father is like someone who wished to slay a prominent person. While still in his own house he drew his sword and thrust it into the wall in order to test whether his hand would be strong enough. Then he slew the prominent person.

99. His Disciples said to him: Your brethren and your mother are standing outside. He said to them: Those here who do my Father's desires are my Brethren and my Mother. It is they who will enter the Kingdom of my Father.

Matthew 12:46 While he was still speaking to the crowds, his mother and his brothers were standing outside, wanting to speak to him. 47 Someone told him, Look, your mother and your brothers are standing outside, wanting to speak to you. 48 But to the one who had told him this, Jesus replied, Who is my mother, and who are my brothers? 49 And pointing to his disciples, he said, Here are my mother and my brothers! 50 For whoever does the will of my Father in heaven is my brother and sister and mother.

100. They showed Jesus a gold coin, and said to him: The agents of Caesar extort taxes from us. He said to them: Give the things of Caesar to Caesar, give the things of God to God, and give to me what is mine.

Mark 12:14 Is it lawful to pay taxes to the emperor, or not? 15 Should we pay them, or should we not? But knowing their hypocrisy, he said to them, Why are you putting me to the test? Bring me a denarius and let me see it. 16 And they brought one. Then he said to them, Whose head is this, and whose title? They answered, The emperor's. 12:17 Jesus said to them, Give to the emperor the things that are the emperor's, and to God the things that are God's. And they were utterly amazed at him.

101. Jesus said: Whoever does not hate his father and his mother as I do, will not be able to become my Disciple. And whoever does not love his Father and his Mother as I do, will

not be able to become my Disciple. For my mother bore me, yet my true Mother gave me the life.

Matthew 10:37 Whoever loves father or mother more than me is not worthy of me; and whoever loves son or daughter more than me is not worthy of me.

102. Jesus said: Damn these Pharisees. They are like a dog sleeping in the feed trough of oxen. For neither does he eat, nor does he allow the oxen to eat.

Matthew 2:.13 But woe unto you, scribes and Pharisees, hypocrites! because you shut the kingdom of heaven against men; for you neither enter yourselves, nor allow those who would enter to go in.

103. Jesus said: Blessed is the person who knows at what place of the house the bandits may break in, so that he can rise and collect his things and prepare himself before they enter.

Matthew 24:43 But understand this: if the owner of the house had known in what part of the night the thief was coming, he would have stayed awake and would not have let his house be broken into.

104. They said to him: Come, let us pray today and let us fast. Jesus said: What sin have I committed? How have I been overcome (undone)? When the Bridegroom comes forth from the Bridal Chamber, then let them fast and let them pray.

105. Jesus said: Whoever acknowledges (comes to know) father and mother, will be called the son of a whore.

106. Jesus said: When you make the two one, you will become Sons of Man (children of Adam), and when you say to the mountain: Move! It will move.

Mark 11:23 Truly I tell you, if you say to this mountain, Be taken up and thrown into the sea, and if you do not doubt in your heart, but believe that what you say will come to pass, it will be done for you.

107. Jesus said: The Kingdom is like a shepherd who has a hundred sheep. The largest one of them went astray. He left the ninety-nine and sought for the one until he found it. Having searched until he was weary, he said to that sheep: I desire you more than the ninety-nine.

Matthew 18:12 What do you think? If a shepherd has a hundred sheep, and one of them has gone astray, does he not leave the ninety-nine on the mountains and go in search of the one that went astray? 13 And if he finds it, truly I tell you, he rejoices over it more than over the ninety-nine that never went astray.

108. Jesus said: Whoever drinks from my mouth will become like me. I will become him, and the secrets will be revealed to him.

109. Jesus said: The Kingdom is like a person who had a treasure hidden in his field and knew nothing of it. After he died, he bequeathed it to his son. The son accepted the field knowing nothing of the treasure. He sold it. Then the person who bought it came and plowed it. He found the treasure. He began to lend money at interest to whomever he wished.

Matthew 13:44 The kingdom of heaven is like treasure hidden in a field, which someone found and hid; then in his joy he goes and sells all that he has and buys that field.

110. Jesus said: Whoever has found the world (system) and becomes wealthy (enriched by it), let him renounce the world (system).

Mark 10:21 Then Jesus beholding him loved him, and said unto him, One thing thou lackest: go thy way, sell whatsoever thou hast, and give to the poor, and thou shalt have treasure in heaven: and come, take up the cross, and follow me. 22 And he was sad at that saying, and went away grieved: for he had great possessions. 23 And Jesus looked round about, and saith unto his disciples, How hardly shall they that have riches enter into the kingdom of God!

111. Jesus said: Heaven and earth will roll up before you, but he who lives within the Living-One will neither see nor fear death. For, Jesus said: Whoever finds himself, of him the world is not worthy.

112. Jesus said: Damned is the flesh which depends upon the soul. Damned is the soul which depends upon the flesh.

113. His Disciples said to him: When will the Kingdom come? Jesus said: It will not come by expectation (because you watch or wait for it). They will not say: Look here! or: Look there! But the Kingdom of the Father is spread upon the

earth, and people do not realize it.

Luke 17:20 And when he was demanded of by the Pharisees, when the kingdom of God should come, he answered them and said, The kingdom of God cometh not with observation: Neither shall they say, Lo-Here! Lo-There! For, behold, the kingdom of God is within you.

(Saying 114 was written later and was added to the original text.)

114. Simon Peter said to them: Send Mary away from us, for women are not worthy of this life. Jesus said: Behold, I will draw her into me so that I make her male, in order that she herself will become a living spirit like you males. For every female who becomes male will enter the Kingdom of the Heavens.

The Tao Te Ching

The Tao Te Ching was written by a man referred to as Lao Tzu. The unknown author's name means both "the old philosopher" and "the old philosophy." Hence Lao Tzu may also be the title for the book or the name or title of the author.

Lao Tzu lived in ancient China and was the keeper of the Imperial Library. Legends tell us he was famous for his wisdom. He was an advocate for personal inner growth, moral government, and the rights of the people. Perceiving the growing corruption of the government, he left for the countryside. On his way, the guard at the city gates asked Lao Tzu to write out his teachings for the benefit of future generations. Lao Tzu wrote the Tao Te Ching, and was never heard of again. The Tao Te Ching is the fundamental text of Taoism.

Taoism is a philosophy based upon the search for a middle path through life; avoiding extremes so that no act is followed by a reaction. This philosophy has come to influence many other aspects of Eastern life; including martial arts in such styles as Tai Chi, Aikido, Shinsei Hapkido, Jujutsu, and Judo.

The concept of balancing the masculine and feminine or hard and soft applied also in Eastern medicines such as herbology and acupuncture.

The practice of Taoism is principally concerned with discovering balance and self-knowledge. All things, actions, and even intents, are broken into positive and negative, or masculine and feminine influences. Taoism advocates learning to sense the world directly, to "intuit" the flow of things, and to maintain a balance of opposing forces.

In doing so, one must contemplate impressions deeply as one attempts to become detached, without resorting to coloring intuitive impressions with personal expectations. Taoism advises against relying on ideologies, because to do so will rob one's life of its meaning and personal intuition. By developing intuition, one acquires a deeper understanding of the world, one's place, and the future. Lao Tzu remarked that an excessive force tends to trigger an opposing force, and therefore the use of force cannot be the basis for establishing a strong and lasting social foundation of control, life, or government. The force used to lead others is said to be the "moral force," virtue, or wisdom of the Master.

There seem to be two theories disputing the dating of the Tao Te Ching. According to tradition, the work originates in the fourth century B.C., but recent discoveries confirm that the writings originate no earlier than the third or fourth century B.C. The oldest existing copy is from 206 or 195 B.C.

The second hypothesis concludes that the teaching may be old enough to pre-date the invention of paper. In fact, its form exhibits many of the features of an oral tradition, suggesting it may pre-date writing as well. Oral traditions are very difficult to trace and we may never know how old the verses are.

The Tao Te Ching, as it exists today, consists of 81 short chapters among which 37 form the first part, the Book of the Way (Tao), and the next 44 form the Book of Te ("Te" is a word translated by James Legge as "virtue", pointing to the Tao of Heaven). Its division into chapters is considered to be the result of the remarks of Heschang Gong (Han dynasty). Other traditional interpretations conclude the name may be "*The Book of the Way of Virtue" or "The Book of Flow and Harmony.*"

Tao Te Ching

1

The Tao that can be explained is not the eternal Tao
The name that can be spoken is not the eternal Name.
The unspeakable is the beginning of everything.
Naming is the origin of every separate thing.
Free from desire, you realize the mystery.
Trapped in desire, you only see the manifestations.
Mystery and manifestations
Arise from the same source.
It is experienced as darkness.
Darkness within darkness.
The gateway to all understanding.

2

When beautiful things appear as beautiful,

It is because other things are called ugly.
We can only know Good because there is Evil.
Having and not having are born together
Being and not being arise from each other.
Difficult and easy support each other.
Long and short define each other.
High and low depend on each other.
Sound and silence harmonize each other.
Before and after follow each other.
Therefore the Master acts without doing anything
And teaches without talking.
He allows things to come and go naturally.
He does not hold on.
He has but doesn't possess, works but takes no credit,
He has no expectations.
It is done and then forgotten, therefore, it lasts forever.

3

If you give some men power, others become powerless.
If you assign value, people begin to steal.
Desire begets confusion of the heart.
The Master leads by emptying people's minds

And filling their hearts,
By weakening their ambition
And toughening their resolve.
He helps people lose everything they know and desire.
Craftiness, ambition, and expectations
Cause things to go badly.
Practice not-doing, and everything will be well.

4

The Tao is like an empty well; used but never emptied.
It is the eternal void and source of all possibilities.
It blunts the sharpness, untangles the knot;
Softens the glare, unifies the dust.
It is hidden deeply but is ever-present.
I don't know from where it came.
It is older than God.

5

The Tao is impartial;
It gives birth to both good and evil.

The Master is impartial

He sees people as both good and evil.

The Tao is like a bellows:

It is empty, changeable, potential in form.

The more it is moved, the more it yields.

The more you talk of it, the less your words count.

Hold on to the stillness of the center.

6

The Tao is called the Great Mother:

Empty yet inexhaustible,

It gives birth to all things.

It is always present within you.

If you use it; it will never fail.

7

Tao is eternal.

Why is it eternal?

It was never born;

Thus, it can never die.

The Master stays behind;

That is why he is ahead.

He is detached from all things;

That is why he is one with all things.

Because he has let go of himself,

He attains fulfillment.

8

The highest good is like water,

Which nourishes all things without trying.

It is content with the low places that people disdain.

Water, goodness and the Tao flow in the same way.

In dwelling, be close to the land.

In thinking, go deep within the heart.

In conflict, be fair and generous.

When speaking, be true.

When ruling, be fair

In work, be competent.

In life, be completely present in each moment.

If there is no fight, there will be no blame.

9

Better to stop short than to fill your bowl to overflowing.
The sharpened knife dulls easily.
Collect money, jewels, and possessions
And you cannot protect them.
Gather wealth and position
And your heart will be their captive.

Do your work, then let it go.
This is the only path to inner peace.

10

Can you control your mind and
Keep it from wandering?
Can you keep your oneness and focus?
Can you let your body become
Supple as a newborn child's?

Can you cleanse your inner vision?
Can you love people and lead them
Without guile or will?
Can you deal with the most vital matters
By letting events take their course?

Can you be lead by Tao,
Keeping an empty mind
And thus being open to all things?

Are you able to be still,
Give birth and nourish,
Create and bear without possessing,
Act without expectations,
Lead without controlling?

This is the highest virtue.

11

Thirty spokes join at the hub of a wheel.
It is the center hole that gives it use.

We shape clay into a pot.
It is the emptiness inside
That makes it useful.

Shape doors and windows for a house.
It is the space that makes it useful.

We derive benefit from things that are there
And usefulness from what is not there.

12

Five colors blind the eye.
Five sounds deafen the ear.
Five flavors dull the taste.
Racing thoughts confuse the mind.
Desires lead the heart astray.

The Master observes the world
But is guided by his intuition.
He allows things to come and go
As they will.

13

Disgrace and success are the same.
Misfortune is a condition of life.

What does it mean to accept disgrace willingly?
Accept not being important.
Do not be concerned with loss or gain.

What does it mean to accept misfortune
As a condition of life?
Misfortune comes to all who are born.
If you had no body, what misery would you have?

Submit to the Tao and you will be trusted with everything.
Love the world as yourself and you can care for all beings.

14

Look for it, and it can't be seen.
Listen for it, and it can't be heard.
Grasp for it, and it can't be held.

These three are beyond understanding,
Thus they as joined as one.
Above, it isn't bright.
Below, it isn't dark.
It is an unbroken, unnamable thread
That returns to the nothingness.
The form is void.
Image without visage,
Beyond definition and imagination.

Examine it. You will see no beginning;
Follow it and there is no end.
With the ancient Tao you will be in the eternal present.
Knowing the beginning is the essence of wisdom.

15

The ancient Masters were profound and subtle.
The depth of their wisdom cannot be measured.
Because they cannot be recognized
We can only describe their appearance.

They were careful

As someone crossing an ice covered stream,
Alert like a warrior in hostile territory,
Courteous as a guest,
Yielding as melting ice,
Simple as a block of wood,
Receptive as a valley,
Clear as a pool of water.

Can you be still inside while the mud settles?
Can you wait quietly until the moment is right?

The Master doesn't seek fulfillment.
Without seeking and without expectations
He is not confused by desires.

16

Empty your mind of every thought.
Let your mind and heart still.
Watch things come and go without attachment.

Everything grows, matures,
And returns to the same source.

Returning to the source is stillness and peace.
This is the way of nature.
It is the way of Tao and it is unchanging.

Not knowing the consistency of Tao
Leads to confusion and disaster.
When you realize the common source
You become tolerant and charitable.
Giving to others, you will be as a king.
Being as a king, you will become divine.
Being divine, you will become one with the eternal Tao.

When death comes, you will be ready
For you will know that the Tao will never pass away.

17

When the Master governs,
The people are hardly aware that he exists.
An ineffective leader is known and loved.
A poor leader is feared.
The worst is one who is despised.

If you don't trust the people, you will not be trusted.

If you do not trust, you make others untrustworthy.

The Master says nothing.

When work is done

The people say, We did it all!

18

When the great Tao is forgotten,

Goodness and piety arise.

When the cleverness and knowledge begin

Falseness and pretension are born.

When there is no peace in the family,

Filial piety and devotion begin.

When the country falls into disarray,

Patriotism is born.

19

Give up trying to be holy or wise,

And people will be a hundred times happier.
Throw away ideas of kindness, morality, and justice,
And people will rediscover love and family.
Give up industriousness and profit,
And there won't be any robbers or thieves.
These three are outward forms and are useless.

Cultivate simplicity.
Realize your true nature.
Renounce selfishness.
Do not desire.

20

Stop thinking, and end your troubles.
What is the difference between yes and no?
What is the difference between success and failure?
Why must I fear what others fear? How ridiculous!

Other people are content with a feast or party
Others are content with a park in spring or a beautiful view.
I alone wonder, uncaring, expressionless as a newborn child.
I have no home.
Other people have what they need;

I alone have nothing.

Others are clear and witty.

I am nothing. My mind is empty.

Other people are bright;

I alone am dim.

Other people are clever;

I alone am dull.

Other people have a purpose;

I am aimless and depressed,

Drifting like a wave on the ocean,

Blown by the wind.

I am different from the others.

I am nourished from the Great Mother.

21

The Master keeps his own mind

And is alone, always at one with the Tao.

The Tao cannot be imagined, yet within is image.

It is elusive and formless, yet within is form.

The Tao is dark and void, yet within is radiance.
The essence is real, yet within is faith.

Since before time was and until now, the Tao is.
How do I know the way of creation is true?
Because of this; I look inside myself and it is there.

22

Yield and overcome;
Bend and be straight;
If you want to become full,
Let yourself be empty.
If you want to be reborn,
Let yourself die.
If you want to be fulfilled,
Give up everything.

Therefore, the Master, resides in the Tao,
And thus sets an example for all.
Because he doesn't put on a display,

People can see his true light.

Because he does not boast,

People can trust his words.

Because he doesn't know who he is,

People recognize themselves in him.

Not bragging or boasting,

There is no quarrel or dissention.

The ancient Masters said,

If you want to receive all,

Give up everything,

Be complete and all things will be yours.

23

To talk a little is natural.

High winds and heavy rains soon exhaust themselves.

If Heaven and Earth cannot sustain then how can man?

He who lives the Tao,

Is in unity with the Tao

He who lives virtuously experiences virtue.

If you lose the Way,

You are willingly lost.

Trust your natural responses;
And everything will be as it should.

24

He who stands on tiptoe is not steady.
He who strives cannot maintain the pace.
He who wishes to be known is not enlightened.
He who defines himself cannot know his true nature.
He who lords over others cannot empower himself.
He who brags will not be remembered.
According to followers of Tao,
These are extra food and unnecessary baggage.
They weigh you down, slow you down and impede your joy.
The followers of Tao reject them.

25

There was something formless and mysterious
Born before anything existed.

It is silent, peaceful, and empty.

Solitary. Unchanging.

Eternally present – peace within motion.

It is the mother of the all things.

It is unnamable.

I call it the Tao.

It flows through all things,

And then returns.

The Tao is great.

The sky is great.

Earth is great.

Man is great.

These are the four great powers.

Man follows the Earth.

Earth follows the sky.

The sky follows the Tao.

The Tao follows only its own natural way.

26

The heavy is the root of the light.
The still is the master of all that moves.

Thus the Master travels all day
Without leaving "home."
However splendid the views,
He stays unattached and calm.

Why should the lord of a country
Flit about like a fool?
If you let yourself be quixotic,
You lose your root.
To be restless or anxious,
Is to lose control and move too soon.

27

A good traveler leaves no tracks.
A good speaker does not stutter.
A good mathematician needs no paper.
A good door needs no lock yet cannot be opened.

A good binding needs no knots yet cannot be untied.

Thus the Master cares for all people
And doesn't reject anyone.
He nurtures all and abandons nothing.
This is called embodying the light.

What is a good man but a bad man's teacher?
What is a bad man but a good man's responsibility?
The teacher is to be respected,
And the student is to be nurtured.
However intelligent you are, if you do not follow
This way there will be confusion.
This is the secret.

28

Know the strength of a man,
Yet keep the heart of a woman:
Let all things flow through you,
Like a true and constant stream.
If you do this, the Tao will never forsake you
And you will be like a little child once more.

Know the white,

Yet keep the black:

Be an example for the world.

If you are an example for the world,

Like a true and constant stream.

You will return, flowing to the All.

Know honor,

Yet have no care for it:

Be the valley of the world.

Being the valley of the world,

All things will flow into you.

Return to the simple state of a block of wood.

Then you will be useful and full of potential.

When the Master uses the Tao he rises above the rest.

Thus a master tailor cuts little.

29

Do you want to improve the world?

I don't think it can be done.

The world is sacred.
It can't be improved.
If you tamper with it, you will ruin it.
If you treat it like a procession, you will lose it.
There are some that are ahead,
And some behind;
Some that are difficult;
And some that are easy;
Some that are weak,
And some that are strong;
Some that will endure,
And some that will be overthrown.

Seek the center path.
Avoid extremes and excess.
Seek balance.
The Master sees and accepts
Without trying to control.

30

If you counsel a warrior about the Tao

Tell him he should not use force.
For every force there is a reaction.
Briars grow where armies tread.
Famine follows in the wake of war.
Do only what needs to be done.
Never take advantage of power.

Achieve results but the results are not your own.
Do not let pride interfere.
Thus, there is nothing to brag about.
Nothing to be proud of.
Nothing to fight about.

Force is followed by weakness.
This is not the Way of the Tao.
Any other way will lead to premature destruction.

31

Weapons are the instruments of violence;
All decent men hate them.

Weapons are the instruments of fear;

A decent man will avoid them until there is no choice.
Peace and serenity are his highest desires.
Victory is no cause for celebration.
For, it you celebrate victory you celebrate death and defeat.
He cannot delight in the slaughter of men.

On happy occasions the underdog is celebrated.
On sad occasions people look to their leaders.
Generals stand to the left, kings and presidents to the right.
Therefore, war is conducted like a funeral
He enters a battle gravely, and has compassion for those killed,
As with a funeral.

32

The Tao cannot be defined.
It is smaller than anything formed,
And cannot be grasped.

If powerful men could use it all things would flow naturally.
Men would do as they should
And the rain would come in its season.

When the whole is divided, all parts must have a name.

Knowing when to stop you can avoid troubles.

All things end in the Tao
As rivers end at the sea.

33

Knowing others is intelligence;
Knowing yourself is wisdom.
Mastering others requires force;
Mastering yourself requires inner strength.

If you realize that you have enough,
You are truly rich.
Tenacity and a perfect finish require willpower.
He who stays centered will endure.
To live in the eternal present one will never die.

34

The great Tao flows everywhere.
All things are born from it and it holds nothing in reserve.

It creates naturally and is not possessive.
It pours itself into its work,
Yet it makes no claim.

It nourishes infinite worlds,
Yet it doesn't hold on to them.

Since it is merged with all things
And is hidden in their hearts,
It can be called humble.
Since all things vanish into it,
It alone endures.
It can be called great.
It isn't aware of its greatness;
Thus it is truly great.

35

All men seek he who is centered in the Tao.
There they find rest, joy, and peace of mind.

Music or the smell of good food
May entice people to stop and enjoy.

But conversations about Tao

Seem boring and bland.

When you look for it, it cannot be seen.

When you listen for it, it cannot be heard.

When you use it, it cannot be exhausted.

36

If you wish to diminish it, allow it to expand.

If you wish to end it, allow it to mature.

If you wish to bash it against the ground, first raise it up.

If you wish to take something, it must first be given.

This is called understanding the nature of things.

The soft overcomes hard.

Weak overcomes strong.

Stay in your element.

Hide your strength until it is needed.

37

The Tao does not strive, yet it leaves nothing undone.

If powerful men observe this Way
The whole world would be as it should be.
If they wanted to act, they would resume
Their simple, everyday lives,
In harmony and free of desire.
Then, there would be peace.

38

A good man does not try to be good. It comes from his heart.
A fool tries to be good but he it is not his natural way.
Therefore, a good man does not strive yet good comes from him.
A fool rushes about trying to act good but no good comes of it.

The kind man acts, kindness leaves nothing lacking.
When a just man acts,
There is judgment and things are left to do.
When the man of discipline follows, no one responds
Until he begins his enforcement.

When the Tao is lost, there is kindness.
When kindness is lost, there is justice.
When justice is lost, there is ritual.

Ritual is the corpse of true faith,
And the beginning of foolishness.

Therefore the Master looks deeply
And is not concerned with how things appear on the surface,

He examines the fruit and not the flower.
He dwells on what is real and not on appearances.

39

From Ancient times, all things arise from the One:
The sky is clear and complete.
The earth is solid and complete.
The spirit is strong and complete.
The valley is full and complete.
All things are alive, complete, and content.

When the Way is not followed,
The sky becomes tarnished,
The earth becomes wasteland,
The spirit is depleted,
Creatures become extinct.

The Master humbly follows the Way, yet seems noble.
He acts as a lowly servant and is thus raised in stature.
Rulers and men of authority feel orphaned, widowed, and alone.
This is humility.
Too much success draws attention like sounding chimes and Rattling jade stones.

40

Returning is the movement of the Tao.
Yielding is the way of the Tao.

All things are born of that which is and was.
Being is born of nothingness.

41

When the seeker hears of the Tao,
He immediately begins to practice it.
When an average man hears of the Tao,
He thinks about it but does not practice it.
When a foolish man hears of the Tao, he laughs out loud.
If he didn't laugh, it wouldn't be the Tao.

Thus it is said:
The path into the light seems dark,
The path forward seems to go back,
The direct path seems prolonged,
The highest good seems empty.
Great purity seems sullied.
Depth of spirit seems inadequate.
True stability seems changeable,
Great talent matures in time.
The highest notes are beyond hearing.
The Tao is obscured and nameless.

It nourishes and completes all things.

42

The Tao created One.

One created Two.

Two created Three.

Three gives birth to all things.

All things carry the feminine

But demonstrate the masculine.

When masculine and feminine are balanced,

Harmony is achieved.

Ordinary men hate being deserted, abandoned, or alone.

But these are how the Master is described.

Embracing his solitude

He becomes aware that he is one with All.

43

The softest thing in the world overcomes the hardest thing.

That which has no substance enters where there is no space.

This shows the value of non-action.

Teaching without words, and acting without movement is the Master's way.

44

Fame or integrity: which is more important?
Integrity or wealth: which do you desire more?
Success or failure: which is more damaging?

If you are attached to processions you will suffer.
If you hoard you will lose.
Contentment assuages disappointment.
Know when to stop, avoid troubles, and remain forever satisfied.

45

Great accomplishments seem imperfect,
But, they continue to be useful.
True fullness seems lacking,
Yet, it is never emptied.

True straightness seems crooked.

True wisdom seems foolish.

True grace seems awkward.

If you are cold, move.

If you are warm, be still.

In stillness and peace, the order of the universe is established.

46

When Tao is present within a country,

Fine horses are free to fertilize the fields.

When Tao is missing in a country,

War horses are bred in the county side.

There is no greater fault than desire,

No worse goad than discontentment.

No greater shame than selfishness

He who realizes enough is enough will be fulfilled.

47

Without traveling you can know the world.

Without looking out of a window,
You can see the ways of the Tao.
The more you go outside yourself the less you understand.

The Master understands without traveling,
Sees the Way without looking,
Achieves without action.

48

In pursuit of knowledge, every day something is added.
In the pursuit of the Tao, every day something is dropped.
Less and less is needed until stillness is achieved.
When nothing is done, nothing is left undone.
If things are left alone they will take their own course.
If you interfere - chaos.

49

The Master has no mind of his own.
He serves the needs of others.

He is good to people who are good.
He is also good to people who are not good.
This is true goodness.

He has faith in people who are trustworthy.
He also has faith in people who are not trustworthy.
This is true trust.

The Master is quiet, timid and does not consider himself.
People do not understand him.
They look and listen even though
They think he behaves like a child

50

In the space of a lifetime,
One third follows the way of life,
One third follows the way of death
And one third follows nothing
And drift through life,
Having no purpose.

He who knows how to live in the Tao

Moves without fear or thought of his actions.
He will not be harmed because there is no place
For weapons or beasts to enter him.
If there is no fear of death,
The mind is clear and death has no place.

51

Everything in existence is an expression of the Tao.
The Tao nurtures them.
Unconsciously and spontaneously, they take on form.
They allow circumstances to shape them.
That is why everything honors the Tao.

The Tao gives birth to all things.
Its goodness nourishes them, protects them, and comforts them.
The Tao does not possess them.
The Tao does not boast of them.
The Tao has no expectations of them.
The Tao guides without interfering.
This is the highest good.

52

Tao is the mother and beginning of all things.
All things issue from it like children from their mother;
And all things return to it.
To know the maker is to know the creation.
Recognize the children and know the mother,
And free yourself from fear and sorrow.

Stay quiet, focus the mind and life will be peaceful.
Speak without thought, entertain desires,
Rush about and your heart will be troubled.

Seeing into darkness and detail is insight.
Yielding is strength.

Use your own light.
Inwardly lighting your own path is wisdom.
Consistence leads to perfection.

53

The center path is the main road.

If I have any sense I will walk the clear path.
But, people prefer the side roads,
Even though the main path is easiest.
Step left or right and things are out of balance.
Stay centered within the Tao.

When rulers demand too much
Common folks lose their land;
When rulers spend money, buy weapons, and distribute wealth
Some wear expensive clothing
Eat fine food, and have many possessions;
While others go hungry.
These rulers are robbers and thieves.
They do not follow the Tao.

54

Whoever is firmly planted in the Tao
Will not be uprooted.
Whoever embraces the Tao
Will not slip away.
His name will be honored
From generation to generation.

Cultivate goodness in your life
And you will become genuine.
Encourage goodness in your family
And your family will flourish.
Spread it throughout your country
And your country will be an example
To the rest of the world.

Let it be present in the universe
And it will be omnipresent.

First, there must be virtue in family, then village,
Then nation, then the world.

How do I know this is true?
By looking.

55

He who is in harmony with the Tao
Is like a newborn child.
Whose bones are soft, its muscles are weak,

Yet its grip is strong.
It doesn't know about sex
Yet its penis can stand erect.
It screams and cries all day long,
Yet never becomes hoarse.
It is in harmony with the Tao.

Harmony brings consistency.
Consistency brings enlightenment.

The Master's power is in his timing.
He lets all things happen without rush or desire;
So he does not exhaust his energies.
He never expects results;
So, he is never disappointed.
What does not follow the Tao will not endure.

56

Those who know don't speak of it.
Those who speak of it do not know it.

Close your mouth,

Guard your senses,
Blunt your sharpness,
Reduce complex problems to basic issues,
Soften your glare,
Let your dust settle.
This is the primal Oneness.

When there is oneness
We will not distinguish between friend or enemy,
Gain or harm, honor or failure.
We will give ourselves continually.

This is the highest state of being.

57

If you want to be a great leader,
You must learn to rule justly.
Do not try to control, allow plans to change on their own.
Rule without striving.

The more laws enacted,
The more cunning people will become.

The more violent the weapons,
The less secure people will be.
The more cunning the people are
The more difficult it is to solve the crimes.

Therefore the Master says:
I let go of the law and ritual,
And people become honest and peaceful.

I do not wage war, and people become prosperous,
I let go of all desire to be a ruler
And the people become good and peaceful.

58

If a country is governed with tolerance,
The people are down to earth and honest.
If people are repressed, they become cunning and crafty.
When happiness is contrived, it is meaningless
Try to make people happy,
And the result is misery.
Try to legislate morality,
And you sow immorality and vice.

Thus the Master is intelligent but not cunning,
To the point but not hurtful.
Straightforward, but not rude.
Radiant, but not blinding.

59

For governing a country and serving the common good,
There is nothing better than moderation.

The moderation comes from laying aside your own ideas.
It depends on wisdom gathered through maturity.
If wisdom is acquired, nothing is impossible.
When possibilities are seen as limitless,
Then, a man is equipped to rule.

Nothing is impossible for him.
Because he has become the mother of all people.
He has deep and solid roots into the Tao.
He will nourish others and have a long, happy life.
He will be able to see the outcome from the beginning.

60

Governing a large country
Is like frying a small fish.
It breaks apart if poked too much.
Too much disturbance leads to damage.

Let Tao be the center
And evil will have no power over you.
Evil exists but can be avoided and does not propagate.

The Master avoids evil.
And thus protects both himself and others.

61

When a country obtains great power,
It becomes like the sea:
All streams run downward into it.
The more powerful it grows,
The greater the need for humility.
Yielding to a smaller country,

The greater country will absorb it.

If the smaller country yields to the greater country

It remains whole and can conquer from within.

Humility means trusting the Tao,

Thus, never needing to be defensive.

It is natural for the lesser to serve and the greater to lead.

It is Virtue for the greater to yield.

62

The Tao is the source of all things.

It is the good man's treasure,

And the bad man's refuge.

Honors can be bought with flattering words,

Respect can be won with good deeds;

The Tao does not choose,

So, do not abandon the bad man.

One day he could be king.

On that day, do not send gifts,

But instead, offer the Tao.

Why did the ancient ones esteem the Tao?

Because, when you seek, you find;

And when you make a mistake, you are forgiven.

Therefore, it is the greatest gift of all.

63

Act without striving;
Work without effort.
See the small as large
And the few as many.
Confront the bitter.
Simplify the complicated.
Attend to details.
Achieve greatness by
Accomplishing small feats.

By doing these things
You will do great things as if they were easy.

Great acts are made of small deeds.
The Master never attempts greatness;
Thus, he achieves greatness.

When there is difficulty, he is not concerned.

He has no preconceived ideas of how things should be.

64

What is rooted is easy to nourish.

What is first beginning is easily stopped.

What is brittle is easy to break.

What is small is easy to scatter.

Prevent trouble before it arises.

Put things in order before there is confusion.

The giant tree the size of a man's arm span

Grows from a small seedling.

A skyscraper begins with a pile of dirt.

The journey of a thousand miles

Starts from beneath your feet.

Rushing into action, you are defeated from the start.

Trying to grasp things, they will slip through your fingers.

Therefore the Master takes no action.

Letting things unfold, he is not defeated.
He does not try to hold anything,
Thus by claiming nothing, he has nothing to lose.

People fail when nearing the end.
The finish should be as strong as the beginning.
Then there will be no failure.

What he desires is non-desire;
He owns nothing but collects nothing.
He has nothing but gives men All.
He helps others find their own nature.
He can care for all things by doing nothing but showing forth the Tao.

65

The ancient Masters
Didn't try to educate the people.
They kept knowledge to themselves.

When people think they know the answers,
They are difficult to guide.

Rulers who use deceit cheat the country.
If you want to learn how to govern,
Avoid being clever or deceitful.
The simplest pattern is the clearest
And easiest to follow.

Cleverness or simplicity; these are the two options.
Understanding this leads to goodness.
The highest good leads all men back to Tao.

66

All streams flow to the sea.
Because it is lower
It receives and rules ten thousand streams.

If the Master would lead,
He must place himself humbly below them.
If you want to lead,
You must learn how to follow.

If a ruler serves the people

No one feels oppressed.

If he stands before the people to guide them,

No one feels manipulated.

The whole world is grateful to him and will not tire of him.

Because he does not compete

He meets with no resistance.

67

Some say that my teaching of the Tao cannot be understood.

Others call it lofty but impractical.

It is different and thus has endured.

I have only three treasures to teach;

Simplicity, patience, and compassion.

Being simple in actions and in thoughts,

You return to the source of being.

Being patient with all,

You are in harmony with the Tao

And care not whether you are ahead or behind others.

In compassion you reconcile all beings and are yourself,
Reconciled.

Lack of compassion is not bravery.
Lack of patience is not spontaneity.
Lack of simplicity is not cleverness
To lack any of these things is certain death.

Compassion brings victory in battle and a steadfast defense.
Heaven saves and guards its own when there is compassion.

68

The best soldier is controlled and thoughtful.
The best general patiently searches the mind of his enemy.
The best businessman serves the good of his clients.
The best victor is merciful.

These embody the virtue of not striving.
They have the gift of knowing others
And thus knowing themselves.
This is in harmony with the Tao.

69

The generals have a saying:
He who moves first loses.
It is better to wait and see.
Better to retreat an inch
Than to take a foot by force.
But, where the enemy leaves an inch, I fill the void.

This is called going forward without seeming to advance;
Attacking without using weapons.

There is no greater misfortune
Than underestimating your enemy.

Underestimating your enemy means vilifying
And lessening him in your mind.

Thus you destroy your three treasures
And become your own worst enemy.

When the battle is joined,
He who is patient and yields, wins.

70

My teachings are easy to understand
And easy to perform.
Yet if you try to practice them you will fail.
If you grasp them they will slip away from you.

My teachings are older than the world.
My actions are from self-knowledge.
Men cannot understand these things
Because they do not seek them within.
Thus, I am abused and they are honored.

The Master wears simple clothes
And holds the treasure within him.

71

Not-knowing is true knowledge.
Ignoring this is sickness.
If you realize that you are sick;

You can start to become healthy.

The Master is sick of being sick
Thus, he has become well.

72

When they lose their sense of awe and mystery,
People turn to religion and law.

When they no longer trust,
If you visit, they are suspicious.
If you offer them work,
They will be wary.
Self-confidence will fail,
And they will become dependant on authority.

Therefore the Master steps back,
So that people won't be confused.
He is not arrogant and does not need to rule.
He lets go and gets out of the way.

73

A brave and driven man will place life on the line.

A brave and patient man will value life.

Of these two, one is good and one is injurious.

Heaven favors certain attributes.

Even the Master does not know why.

The Tao does not try but it covers the whole world.

It asks no questions but is answered to by all.

It is not petitioned but supplies every need.

It has no observable goal but fulfills all that is required.

The Tao casts its net wider than the world.

Though the mesh is large, it holds and keeps all things.

74

If men are not afraid to die,

There is nothing that can stop them.

Law is upheld by fear of punishment.

But who wants to be the executioner?

If you take his place you will harm yourself.

It is like trying to take the place of a master carpenter.

If you use his tools,

You may cut your hand.

75

When taxes are too high, people go hungry.

When the government is too restrictive, people soon rebel.

When the price of life becomes too high,

People think of death more often.

Having little to live on, or few things to live for,

The value of life falls.

76

Men are born soft and supple;

Dead, they are stiff and hard.

Green plants are tender and pliant;

When they die they become brittle, brown, and dry.

Thus whoever is stiff and inflexible

Is a disciple of death.

Whoever is soft and yielding

Is a disciple of life.

A tree that will not bend will be broken.

Tactics of life should be fluid to meet changing circumstance.

Flow with change or meet defeat.

For the hard and unyielding will be broken.

The soft and yielding will prevail.

77

As the Tao acts, it is like the bending of a bow.

The high is bent downward;

The low is raised up.

It adjusts excess and deficiency of strength,

Measure, and status

And blends all into harmony and balance.

The Tao takes from those with more and gives
To those with less.
Man's ways are the opposite.
Man esteems those who are wealthy and shuns
Those with little.
Only the Tao gives what it has.

The Master produces without owning,
Works without credit, succeeds without plaudits.
He is not proud or arrogant.

78

Nothing in the world is as soft and yielding as water.
Yet it wears down the hard and inflexible.
Nothing can withstand it.

The weak overcomes strong;
Gentle overcomes the rigid.
Everyone knows this but few practice it.

Therefore the Master knows

That only he who takes on the hardship of the people
Is fit to rule them.

And he who does not shield himself from common disaster
Is fit to rule a country.

True words seem paradoxical.

79

After a fight, resentment remains.
It cannot be helped.

Therefore, the Master fulfills his promises,
Corrects his own mistakes,
And has no expectations of others.

When there is honor, one does his part.
When there is no honor, one makes demands.
The Tao is everywhere,
But it rests on the good man.

80

If a country has few inhabitants,
They enjoy their work,
They don't need complicated machinery,
They love their homes,
They aren't interested in travel.

There are wagons and boats left unused,
Armor that is never worn.
People enjoy their simple ways, food, and clothes.

They live in peace with their neighbor.
Dogs bark and roosters crow and all is heard for miles away.

They are content to grow old and die without
Straying from their ways.

81

True words are not pleasing;
Pleasing words are not true.
Wise men don't need to prove their point;

Men who push their point are fools.

Those who know they could be wrong are learned.

Those who are certain they know are ignorant.

The Master has no possessions.

He hoards nothing.

The more he gives, the more he has.

The more he serves, the happier he is.

The Tao pierces the heart but does not harm.

The Tao nourishes by letting go.

***By not dominating, the Master's obligation is do*ne.**

CPSIA information can be obtained
at www.ICGtesting.com
Printed in the USA
LVHW021459310321
683084LV00009B/863

9 781933 580586